*TWAYNE'S WORLD AUTHORS SERIES*

*A Survey of the World's Literature*

Sylvia E. Bowman, Indiana University

GENERAL EDITOR

# GERMANY

Ulrich Weisstein, Indiana University

EDITOR

## Frank Wedekind

( TWAS 55 )

## TWAYNE'S WORLD AUTHORS SERIES (TWAS)

*The purpose of TWAS is to survey the major writers
—novelists, dramatists, historians, poets, philosophers,
and critics—of the nations of the world. Among the
national literatures covered are those of Australia,
Canada, China, Eastern Europe, France, Germany,
Greece, Italy, Japan, Latin America, New Zealand,
Poland, Russia, Scandinavia, Spain, and the African
nations, as well as Hebrew, Yiddish, and Latin Classical literature. This survey is complemented by
Twayne's United States Authors Series and
English Authors Series.*

*The intent of each volume in these series is to present
a critical-analytical study of the works of the writer;
to include biographical and historical material that
may be necessary for understanding, appreciation,
and critical appraisal of the writer; and to present all
material in clear, concise English—but not to vitiate
the scholarly content of the work by doing so.*

# Frank Wedekind

By SOL GITTLEMAN

*Tufts University*

Twayne Publishers, Inc.    ::    New York

TO ROBYN ALONE

# *Preface*

The aim of this book is a simple and direct one: to introduce a generally unheralded German literary figure to the American public. There is as yet no other full-length study in English of Frank Wedekind, whom Block and Shedd call "the least popular major dramatist of our time." Wedekind has always been a dramatist's dramatist, exerting a considerable international influence on the modern theater while remaining, for the most part, unrecognized as a creator.

Wedekind's role in the intellectual revolution in Germany and Europe around the turn of the century has never been fully appreciated. As a personality and literary celebrity, he generated an excitement far greater than his more famous contemporary and compatriot, Gerhart Hauptmann, and, in the long run, exercised a far greater influence on the future direction of the theater. As a writer who is in constant conflict with his age, Wedekind has no equal. His involvement with his times makes at least a brief biographical chapter essential. Yet, it would be a terrible injustice to Wedekind if this were the only reason for considering his life in relationship to his art; for his life *was* his art and actually served as the raw material for most of his plays. Few writers have been as blatantly autobiographical as Wedekind.

I am indebted to the editors of the *German Quarterly* and *Modern Drama* for permission to quote from two of my published articles, "The Image of America in the Works of Frank Wedekind" and "Bertolt Brecht and Frank Wedekind: Notes on a Literary Relation." I should also like to thank the Albert Langen-Georg Müller Verlag in Munich for granting permission to quote from the two editions of Wedekind's works.

The translations, unless otherwise indicated, are my own.

S. G.

# Contents

# Chronology

1849    Friedrich Wilhelm Wedekind settles in San Francisco as a practicing physician. Politically active as a spokesman for German liberalism.

1862    Marriage to Emilie Kammerer, German-born opera singer, twenty-four years his junior. Family moves to Oakland, California. Birth of first son, Arnim.

1864    The Wedekinds return to Germany for what is planned as a brief visit. On July 24, birth of Benjamin Franklin Wedekind in Hanover.

1872    Family leaves Germany because of Dr. Wedekind's continued political disenchantment with Bismarck. Purchase of Schloss Lenzburg near Aarau in Switzerland.

1875    Frank attends the regional school in Lenzburg.

1877    First dramatic effort, *Eine Szene aus dem Orient, 8 Akte, Verfasser Dr. F. Wedekind,* age thirteen.

1879    Frank at the Gymnasium in Aarau, is considered an American visitor by classmates. Center of a "Dichterbund" among his friends. First writings on theme of love. Correspondence with Olga Plümacher, "die philosophische Tante" and introduction to philosophical pessimism.

1882    Earliest poems. Wedekind known to friends as "Der Bänkelsänger."

1884    Graduated with "Abitur," Frank begins study of German and French literature at Lausanne, later at Münster. At the wish of his father he undertakes study of law. An avid theatergoer.

1886    *Der Schnellmaler oder Kunst und Mammon,* published in 1889 by Schabelitz in Zürich, his first serious dramatic work. Decides to dedicate himself to writing, in spite of father's disapproval. In Munich Frank meets Michael Georg Conrad and other German "Zolaisten," but immediately rejects theories of Naturalism. Close friendship with Karl Henckell, an active

Naturalist and Socialist. Violent argument with father forces Frank to leave his family. Moves to Zurich, where he is employed as advertising head for the Maggi Corporation.

1887    Articles for the *Neue Zürcher Zeitung.* Comedy in verse, *Elins Erweckung.* Membership in *Das junge Deutschland,* organization of writers under attack by the German government. In Zurich he meets the expatriate German writers Carl and Gerhart Hauptmann. Reconciliation with father.

1888    Death of father in October. Inheritance gives Frank a measure of financial freedom.

1889    In Berlin continued association with Naturalists, especially Otto Hartleben. Completion of *Die junge Welt,* a comic satire of Naturalism, the Woman's Emancipation Movement, and a personal attack on Gerhart Hauptmann.

1891    In Munich a member of *Gesellschaft für modernes Leben,* friendship with Otto Julius Bierbaum. Close association with Willi Morgenstern, born Rudinoff, internationally known clown and pantomimist. *Die junge Welt* published as *Kinder und Narren.* Publication of *Frühlings Erwachen.* At end of the year first trip to Paris.

1892    Total immersion in Parisian night life. Closest friends are Rudinoff, the weight-lifter Holtoff, and the clown Duroff. Completion of *Fritz Schwigerling,* later published as *Der Liebestrank.* Friendship with Emma Herwegh, widow of poet Georg Herwegh.

1894    Several months in London. Acquaintance with Max Dauthendey, German neo-Romantic poet. Back in Paris, secretary to Willi Gretor, a Danish forger and art dealer. Introduced to Albert Langen, the German publisher. Completion of *Das Sonnenspektrum* and work on *Lulu.*

1895    Langen publishes *Erdgeist.* Harassment by German censor because of *Frühlings Erwachen* and *Erdgeist.* In Berlin the *Freie Bühne* rejects *Erdgeist* for production.

1896    Again in Munich, Wedekind involved in founding of *Simplizissimus.* Love affair with Frieda Strindberg, who is about to divorce the Swedish dramatist.

1897    Birth of a son, Friedrich Strindberg. Appearance of prose, poetry, and pantomimes in *Fürstin Russalka.* Completion of *Der Kammersänger.*

1898    Engaged by the *Ibsen-Theatre* in Leipzig as director and actor. February first production of a Wedekind play, *Erdgeist,* with Wedekind as Dr. Schön. Beginning of his acting career. Georg Stollberg invites him to *Münchner Schauspielhaus*. Because of anti-government poems in *Simplizissimus* Wedekind must flee the country.

1899 Completion of *Marquis von Keith*. In June returns to Leipzig to face charges of "Majestätsbeleidigung." Imprisonment. In prison completes *Mine-Haha*, a novel.

1900 Released from jail in March and returns to Munich. Friendship with Max Halbe. Wedekind active as performer in his own plays and the repertoire of the *Münchner Schauspielhaus*.

1901 Opening of the cabaret *Elf Scharfrichter* in Munich, with Wedekind singing to his own guitar accompaniment. Accepted as an idol by the Bohemians.

1902 *So ist das Leben* (*König Nicolo*), Wedekind's first completely "confessional" play. Appearance in *Marquis von Keith*, with strong critical reaction, pro and con.

1903 *Hidalla, oder Karl Hetmann, der Zwergriese. Der Kammersänger* becoming a popular repertory piece throughout Germany.

1905 First Wedekind cycle, in Nürnberg. Karl Kraus produces a revision of the second part of the original *Lulu* material, *Die Büchse der Pandora*. Wedekind finishes *Totentanz*, published as *Tod und Teufel*, so as not to conflict with Strindberg's play.

1906 Marriage to Tilly Newes, a young actress. Max Reinhardt gives premiere of *Frühlings Erwachen* in *Deutsches Theater*, Berlin, starring the Wedekinds. Sudden success of his other plays. *Tod und Teufel* banned. Birth of daughter, Pamela. Completion of *Musik*.

1907 *Die Zensur*.

1908 In *Oaha, Die Satire der Satire*, Wedekind attacks Albert Langen.

1909 Wedekind appears in a seven-play cycle of his works in Munich.

1910 *Schloss Wetterstein* appears, and there is further difficulty with the censor.

1911 Birth of a second daughter, Kadidja. Wedekind completes his "Faust play," *Franziska*.

1914 Wedekind honored on his fiftieth birthday as the symbol of literary freedom. Publication of *Das Wedekindbuch*, with contributions from every leading German literary figure, with the exception of Gerhart Hauptmann. *Simson.*

1916 *Bismarck.* Most active as a guest performer in his own plays. Essays seem to condone Germany's involvement in war, after a lifelong commitment to pacifism and antimilitarism. In Zurich, the *Café Voltaire* is opened and *Dadaism* is born. On the first program Wedekind's songs are sung.

1917 *Herakles,* a biblical verse tragedy.

1918 Wedekind dies on March 9th, after an operation. Burial in Munich, attended by thousands of notables and Bohemians. Brecht's obituary appears in *Augsburger Neueste Nachrichten,* March 12.

"Wedekind, history will one day say, was in this partly senile, partly puerile, partly feminine epoch—its only man."

Thomas Mann

# CHAPTER 1

## Eros and Sexus

GIVEN the nature of Frank Wedekind's argument with civilization, it is not surprising that he became one of the most controversial figures in the history of German literature. He was a most "unpleasant" writer. Wedekind was the first German writer, indeed, almost the first western writer, to use Freud's thesis that "civilization is based on the permanent subjugation of the human instincts."[1] Now, no society likes to think of itself as subjugating its instincts, and the society of Wedekind's time took his insinuation as a direct attack—just as it was intended. But Wedekind was always an "engaged" writer, and his conflict with the world around him was clearly brought on by him quite intentionally. Like his spiritual mentor Friedrich Nietzsche, Wedekind wanted a changed order, a liberated society free from the limitations of a traditional, repressive culture, one uninhibited by taboos. He rejected a world order which, he felt, had for centuries cultivated man the worker, not man the pleasure-seeker.

Wedekind sought for a new kind of relationship between the human being and his biological instincts, which, he insisted, had become incompatible with one another, in the light of civilized society. He hoped to show that mankind's energies needed redirection, back to a more primitive, instinctive form which would allow for a freer, more natural, fundamentally more honest life.

Like Freud, Wedekind grew to believe that the idea of a nonrepressive civilization was impossible. At the heart of his idea of the utopian society was the liberation of mankind from his sexual restraint. Eros, the life-instinct, must be given freedom from the restraints of a civilization which is fundamentally opposed to it as a result of thousands of years of conditioning. At the outset of his career, Wedekind held out hope that Eros could overcome the inhibited society. His symbol of the unrestricted sexual force was "Das

[ 1 ]

Freudenmädchen," a creature free of the moral limitations of the society around her, who in her harmonious existence cries out an "Everlasting Yea" to life. Her state of blissful equilibrium attests to Wedekind's faith in the feasibility of such a life. He considered the erotic drive in such a woman as a satiable need, one which could find complete contentment when given the freedom to act. In the fragmentary dramatic "idyll" *Das Sonnenspektrum* Wedekind created an ideal pleasure palace of sensualism, with exotic love gardens filled with dancing young girls offering unrestrained happiness to the overcivilized young men who seek their company. Eros here is humane and offers to the product of an inhibited world the hope for an instinctively honest existence. The people in this idealized bordello are genuinely contented: "Here one cries only tears of joy."[2] In most of his earlier works Wedekind forcefully advocates this belief in the redemptive power of, for want of a better word, sex.

Later, with the sexual drive embodied in his most memorable creation, Lulu, Eros comes into monumental conflict with civilization, as Freud had indicated that it must. In the two Lulu plays, *Erdgeist* and *Die Büchse der Pandora*, Wedekind's reincarnation of this mythic life-force destroys the several men who lust after her. In its encounter with civilization which cannot really comprehend it, Eros become a destructive principle. What had been a harmonious existence blessed with the sensual tranquillity of the erotic experience turns into a death experience with Lulu, who as the personification of Eros is no longer compatible or "desirable" for the well-being of a society which is now alien to her. Lulu and society cannot function together, and the collision of the two causes an irreconcilable conflict. Civilization is quick to recognize this, and the conflict enters a new phase in *Die Büchse der Pandora*. Society is no longer on the defensive, no longer the hapless victim of a power beyond its ability to understand. Lulu, the beautiful, hypnotic creature of *Erdgeist* is transformed into a hunted, frightened animal. Finally, driven to a debased prostitution, she fatalistically accepts her death at the hands of a sexual pervert in a wretched garret. When Lulu is destroyed by Jack the Ripper, society symbolically has taken its revenge on the sexual life-force.[3]

Freud had in his favor the objectivity of the scientific approach. If he viewed civilization's progress as the natural development of repression, this thesis would cause a stir, but the very detachment of the scientist could act as a shield. The reaction, however, to Wedekind's approach to the same issue, was something else again.

[ 2 ]

He spent his entire life attempting to clear his name of the charge of pornography. In the eyes of the entrenched power structure of Germany, which consisted of the middle class, the church, and the government, Wedekind's ideas were absolutely satanic and menaced the very existence of society. It was as if "civilization had to defend itself against the specter of a world which could be free."[4]

The savagery of the public's attack on Wedekind and his works was unprecedented in the Germany of his age. By defaming him the civilized world was apparently attempting to protect itself from what it considered the disruptive forces which he begged them to recognize. The full force of civilized morality was mobilized against Wedekind and against the taboos which it refused to confront. For Wedekind, Eros was the road to a higher culture; for the society to which he addressed himself, it was an obscenity.

CHAPTER 2

# The Poet in Revolt

IT has been said that the first forty years of Frank Wedekind's life consisted of one continuous battle with the world. Everything about him was unconventional and dissonant. While his contemporaries Emile Zola and Gerhart Hauptmann cried out against the social injustices of the age and sought to convey their message through environmentally conditioned Naturalism, Wedekind preached a doctrine of "Lebensgenuss" based on a revival of spiritual sensuality and bodily pleasure. In the face of rooted Victorian propriety, he championed freedom of the flesh and advocated what seemed to most no more than unrestricted licentiousness. With a Nietzschean fervor he attacked the moral standards of a society which inhibited man's natural instincts. All of this Wedekind expressed in a dramatic idiom which defied every doctrine of the dominant literary movement of his day.

When Wedekind died in March, 1918, at the age of fifty-four, he had already fallen victim to the popular judgment which was to dog his reputation for the next half-century. To the large majority of critics and general readers, Wedekind's writings represented the sexual mania in literature, the product of an asocial, Bohemian character whose works reflected a morbid preoccupation with sex, lust, and perversion. Just as Anton Chekhov was to suffer from the interpretation that his plays were solely the expression of the twilight mood of a wistfully declining nobility, Wedekind's efforts were viewed, labeled, and condemned from one perspective.

His private and public life, moreover, strengthened this image. He loved to play the Bohemian, and as a young writer in search of recognition, Wedekind blithely scandalized bourgeois society. He consciously cultivated a Mephistophelian posture, delighted in associating with the demimonde of forgers, circus people, and prostitutes, and at a time when his plays were receiving scant attention, his

[ 4 ]

name was constantly exposed to the public through assorted trials, litigations, and numerous confrontations with the censors.

If, like his literary predecessors Lenz, Büchner, and Grabbe, Wedekind had died before his full artistic maturity had developed, the world would have had little reason to consider him other than that which he seemed to be: an outcast, a notorious nonconformist, a sexually possessed exhibitionist. But Wedekind did live out his life and developed a plethora of ideas which demonstrate that he deserves a more objective treatment. For if there ever was an individual in advance of his times, it was Frank Wedekind. Along with August Strindberg he was the world's first consciously Freudian dramatist, and to a much greater extent than his Swedish contemporary he devoted himself to the impact of a repressive civilization on the instinctive Eros in mankind. The effect of dealing with this highly sensitive subject matter on Wedekind's reputation was decisive. He became, as one contemporary noted, "the terror of all moralists and every middle-class convention."[1] The Wedekind stigma even spread to his associates. The noted scholar Artur Kutscher, one of Germany's outstanding theater historians, befriended Wedekind and invited him to lecture at his seminar at the University of Munich, for which Kutscher was severely rebuked by the university officials. It was regarded as an academic scandal that as a result of his three-volume critical biography of Wedekind Kutscher was never promoted to "ordentlicher Professor."

For most of his life, Wedekind was a fighter for unpopular causes. As a pacifist, internationalist, and passionate believer in individual freedom, he was admired most by the avant-garde who saw in the government's attack on his plays an effort to stifle the expression on the nonconformist. Even in his later years, when his artistic abilities had diminished considerably and the flare of his youthful exuberance had given way to a happy marriage, parenthood, and an acceptance of many of those values which he had originally detested, Wedekind remained a source of inspiration for a new group of young Bohemians, led by Bertolt Brecht. There existed a mystique which one senses in the obituary written by Brecht just after Wedekind's death in 1918:

A few weeks ago at the Bonbonniere he sang his songs to guitar accompaniment in a brittle voice, slightly monotonous and quite untrained. No singer ever gave me such a shock, such a thrill. It was the man's intense aliveness, the energy which allowed him to defy sniggering ridicule and proclaim his brazen hymn to humanity, that also gave him this personal magic.

In the autumn, when a small group of us heard him give a reading of *Herakles,* his last work, I was amazed at his brazen energy. For two and a half hours without a break, without even dropping his voice (and what a strong brazen voice it was!), without even a moment's breather between acts, bent motionless over the table, he recited partly by heart, those verses wrought in brass, looking deep into the eyes of each of us in turn as we listened to him. . . . Without actually seeing him buried, I cannot conceive that he is dead. Like Tolstoy and Strindberg, he was one of the great educators of modern Europe. His greatest work was his own personality.[2]

## I  *The American Heritage*

Wedekind was marked as an outsider even before his birth. Indeed, from the point of view of national origin, Wedekind's heritage is unique in German literary history. To this day it is not certain whether he died as a German, Swiss, or American citizen. His father, Friedrich Wilhelm Wedekind, had studied medicine in Göttingen and soon after completing his training traveled east in search of adventure. He served as medical officer in the Turkish government and participated in several expeditions to the Tigris and Euphrates. Returning to Germany, Dr. Wedekind became an active supporter of liberal constitutional reform. As an activist and pamphleteer, he was an outspoken advocate of the assembly in the Paulskirche. After the wrecking of the liberals' dreams of a democratic Germany, Wedekind felt that he could not longer live in his homeland; and in 1849 he emigrated to the United States, setting up his medical practice in San Francisco. In 1860 he received as a patient Emilie Kammerer, herself the daughter of a political agitator who had fled Switzerland in 1838. Emilie had come to America in 1856 and earned her living as a singer in a touring German opera company. Dr. Wedekind, who was most active in American-German affairs in the San Francisco area, took more than a medical interest in his young patient, who was twenty-four years his junior, and introduced her into the social world of the expatriate German community. Emilie, who was separated from her husband, married Wedekind in 1862, when her divorce became finalized. They moved into a new home in Oakland, across the bay from San Francisco, and were naturalized as American citizens soon afterwards. In January, 1863, their first child, Arnim, was born.

In 1864 the Wedekinds decided to pay a visit to their native Germany. Soon after their arrival in Hanover, Mrs. Wedekind gave birth to a second son, and in honor of their newly adopted country, he was named Benjamin Franklin. It would seem that the Wedekinds clearly intended to return to America at the time, for in the baptismal registry of Sankt Ägidien's in Hanover the following entry appears after Frank's name: "The child will accompany the parents unbaptised on the return trip to California."[3] As a family the Wedekinds never returned to the United States, and from that day on Frank's actual nationality was a cause of great confusion and considerable personal pain. According to Kutscher the father insisted that the male Wedekind children be considered American citizens, since he did not want them to serve as "Kanonenfutter" in the Prussian army.[4] In 1872, still violently anti-royalist, Dr. Wedekind took his growing family from what he felt was the intolerable oppression of Germany and settled in Switzerland, where he purchased Schloss Lenzburg in the canton of Aarrau, near the district's principal city of the same name. There were now five children, with the arrival of William Lincoln in 1866, Frieda Marianne Erika in 1868, and Donald Lenzelin in 1871. The last to arrive was Emilie, born in 1876. Throughout his early schooldays, Frank was regarded, by friends and officials alike, as "Frank Wedekind aus San Francisko" and enjoyed the status of a visiting dignitary. For Frank and his family it was a foregone conclusion that the boys were American citizens. Yet many years later Frank was expelled from Berlin because he could not produce sufficient documentation to prove his American citizenship. As late as 1898 the problem had not been solved. While awaiting trial in Leipzig on a charge of "Majestätsbeleidigung" he wrote to a friend: "Now I can hope to take advantage of this misfortune so that I might finally gain an official nationality. It's not my fault that I don't have one yet."[5]

America became for Frank a preoccupation. During almost every phase of his life, he found himself exposed to influences from the New World. At home, as the elder Wedekind grew more and more irascible and bitter toward reactionary Germany, he held up the American Federalist system as the most exemplary form of government for guaranteeing the individual's freedom.

But even more important for young Franklin's intellectual growth was the impact of a relative living in the United States. His maternal aunt, "die philosophische Tante" Olga Plümacher, was by far the most significant influence in the development of Wedekind's earliest ideas.

Olga Plümacher was a woman of unusual intelligence. A student

of philosophy, she was one of the outstanding interpreters of philosophical pessimism, especially that system espoused by Eduard von
Hartmann, the late nineteenth-century eclectic and one of the more
lucid followers of Schopenhauer. Miss Plümacher's earliest studies of
von Hartmann's views were written while she lived in the Cumber-
land Mountains of Tennessee in the 1870's, and Wedekind's extensive
correspondence with her dates from that period. Besides instructing
her nephew in the deterministic "Weltschmerz" concepts of von
Hartmann's vision, she introduced Frank to a school of writers whom
she associated with these ideas: Nicolaus Lenau, Heinrich Heine,
Lord Byron, and the German Romantic dramatists Christian Dietrich
Grabbe and Georg Büchner, both of whom were to have a direct
influence on Wedekind's dramatic writings from the very outset of
his literary career.

Olga Plümacher was not the only member of the family to spend
time in America. Frank's two brothers William and Donald both
traveled to the United States, William in 1886 and Donald two years
later. Each in turn found America hostile and returned to Europe
thoroughly disenchanted. Frank yearned to make the journey himself, but never was able to. As a result—and in spite of the disillusionment of his brothers—a particular idea evolved in his mind, that
of America as a land of unattainable freedom and opportunity. In
the plays *Frühlings Erwachen* (*Spring's Awakening*), *Die Büchse
der Pandora* (*Pandora's Box*) and in the short story "Der Brand von
Egliswyl" ("The Burning of Egliswyl"), America offers three desperate individuals hope of escape from persecution, and characteristically in each case this escape is denied them. This theme appears in
a lighter tone in a poem written while Wedekind was working for
the famous satirical magazine *Simplizissimus* and entitled "Der
Deutsch-Amerikanische Handelsvertrag" ("The German-American
Trade Agreement"). Addressing his remarks to a female superior,
the author suggests that he would be just the right person to send
to the United States for the purpose of arranging the treaty:

> Deshalb bitte ich, Ew. Jungfräulichkeit möge geruhen,
> Mir recht viel Geld in meinen Beutel zu tuen
> Und mich zu entsenden nach Amerika,
> Denn es erwachsen uns jetzt grosse Vorteile da.
>
> Mit dem reichsten amerikanischen Schweineschlächter
> Schliesse ich dann als geborner politischer Nachtwächter

> Einen Handelsvertrag ab, nach dessen erstem Artikul
> Es mir seine Tochter gibt zum ehelichen Gemuhl.[6]
> (VIII, 141)

The tone is mildly satirical of the bumbling German trade commissions, but several of the quatrains reveal Wedekind's sensitivity about his citizenship and his difficulties in proving, as he still insisted, that he was indeed an American:

> Paragraph drei: Hat einer amerikanisches Bürgerrecht erworben
> Dann behalt er solches so lange, bis er gestorben,
> Ausgenommen, dass er deutscher Abkunft sei;
> Dann ist es mit dem Bürgerrecht schon vorher vorbei.
>
> Nun aber kommt der wichtigste der Paragraphen:
> Deutschland verbietet bei den schwersten Strafen,
> Dass sich irgend jemand in dieser Welt
> Für einen Deutsch-Amerikaner hält,
>
> Und ahndet es als ein schlimmes Verbrechen,
> Wenn Deutsche in Amerika ihre Muttersprache sprechen.
> Dagegen bleibt für Amerika die Vergünstigung bestehen,
> Dass es hierüber lässt Gnade für Recht ergehen.
> (VIII, 142–43)

Written in 1899, the verse reflects the continued search for a national identity by Wedekind. He did not personally experience difficulties as a native speaker of German in America, but the problem was genuine for his brothers, and especially for one of his closest friends, the composer Hans Richard Weinhöppel, who had just returned from an extended visit to the United States. For all its easy humor and banter, the major theme of the work is the author's desire to be sent to America with all dispatch:

> Versehen Sie mich deshalb in möglichster Bälde
> Für meine Amerikafahrt mit dem nötigen Gelde.
> (VIII, 143)

It was also to America that Wedekind looked for a liberal attitude toward morality. In the plays *Die junge Welt* and *Hidalla, oder Karl Hetmann der Zwergriese* (*Karl Hetmann, the Dwarf Giant*) America is a sort of Promised Land of free-wheeling social reform which permits experimentation in matters of love and marriage forbidden in Europe.

*[ 9 ]*

Wedekind had an almost eccentric curiosity for Americans and things American. Paradoxically, in spite of his enthusiasm for America in the abstract, he was distinctly critical of Americans in the flesh. In his works they are a despicable group of insensitive exploiters (*Der Liebestrank* [*The Love Potion*], *Bethel*), lust murderers (*Schloss Wetterstein* [*Castle Wetterstein*], and boors (*Hidalla, Oaha*). Throughout the plays and poetry there are constant references to famous Americans (Rockefeller, Carnegie, Edison, Buffalo Bill, Gentleman James Corbett, Theodore Roosevelt) as well as a particularly antic use of American Indian names, such as "Oaha" and "Mine-Haha." While writing for *Simplizissimus*, one of his favorite pseudonyms was Cornelius Mine-Haha!

This strange American dream, part romance, part enlightenment, and part "Unkultur," was a significant aspect of Wedekind's creative imagination and gives his writings a quality heretofore unknown in German literature. It marks the beginning of the "Americanization" of German letters, a critical curiosity of the New World which, in twentieth-century writers such as Brecht, Friedrich Dürrenmatt, and Günter Grass, turns into a major influence.

## II  *Die Wanderjahre*

As a student in the "Gymnasium" in Aarau, Frank had already established himself at the center of a group of young comrades who had formed a "Dichterbund." Wedekind, like Melchior Gabor in *Frühlings Erwachen*, was obviously the product of an enlightened home environment. His mother's sensitive understanding contributed as much to his youth as did his father's explosive liberalism, and the family often spent evenings together in lively discussions about the problems of youth, the lack of sympathy of the older generation, and literature. It was only natural that Frank should be a leader among his peers, since he brought into his school experience the passionate intellectualism which he found at home. The mood of these adolescents was that of the serious, searching youth in *Frühlings Erwachen*, with all the accompanying problems and tensions of that children's tragedy. Life for Frank and his friends was a series of conflicts with school authorities which represented the worst aspect of the educational system of the times. Between 1883 and 1885, two of his friends committed suicide, and when he himself graduated in 1884 he had already dedicated himself to a lifelong struggle to change the order of things which had left an indelible impression of dullness, pedantry, and brutality on him. It was this impression which was to furnish the material for his first major literary effort almost a decade later.

After a brief stay at Lausanne, Wedekind arrived in Munich with his brother Arnim, with strict instructions from his father that he undertake the study of law. Frank accepted his father's dictum, not wanting to irritate him. Dr. Wedekind was beginning to show signs of eccentricity. His bitterness against all aspects of totalitarianism grew into a distemper and moodiness which gradually cut him off from the rest of the family. He would roam the top floor of Schloss Lenzburg behind locked doors, allowing visitors only to fulfill his wishes, which he indicated by banging his foot on the floor. When Frank suggested that he might like to study literature in Munich, Dr. Wedekind exploded, but his wife interceded and forestalled a family argument.

The intellectual atmosphere of Munich had the anticipated effect on Frank. The theater and ballet occupied most of his time, at the expense of his law studies, which proved to be as boring as he had imagined. He demonstrated, however, a great interest in Arnim's medical curriculum, especially in the lectures in gynecology. Even his earliest verse written during his schooldays at Aarau betrayed a more than casual curiosity about "Das Weibliche." These Heine-like lyrics were generally bucolic, more often sentimental, and always delicately erotic. In Munich, this youthful outpouring of emotionalism gave way to a more mature and clinical attitude toward the physiology of the female sex. Wedekind was beginning to formulate in his mind the role of woman in society.

For the aspiring young writer, Munich was indeed a center of gravity. It was there that the rumblings of a profound literary revolution could be heard, and Wedekind instinctively made his way to the source of this action. Through the influence of a friend from Lenzburg, Karl Henckell, he was introduced to those literary figures who represented the new Zolaism, as it was called. Henckell, himself a writer, was already an active disciple when he met Wedekind in the summer of 1885. His *Poetisches Skizzenbuch* appeared that year with a foreword by Heinrich Hart, who was one of the leading theoreticians of the new movement. Along with Hermann Conradi, another of the Zolaists, Henckell wrote the elaborate introduction to *Moderne Dichtercharaktere*, which was one of the first anthologies to popularize the new writers.

These were, of course, the literary exponents of what has come to be known as the Naturalistic movement. Through Henckell Wedekind was introduced to one of the key figures, Michael Georg Conrad, founder of the most influential literary organ devoted to the publication of avant-garde material, *Die Gesellschaft, realistische Zeitschrift für Litteratur, Kunst und öffentliches Leben*. Wedekind listened and studied, as he attempted to evaluate the literary credo of the Naturalists, their unique "Sekundenstil" of reportorial description, the scientific detachment of the writer vis-à-vis his material, and the new militancy in matters of social inequality. Politically, the new Naturalism attracted him, for Wedekind was already a passionate enemy of social injustice. But almost from the outset he felt out of sympathy with the artistic and intellectual restrictions of Naturalism. In a sense, he had already transcended its frame of reference and what seemed to him a commitment to a society-oriented world. Wedekind did not want to work *within* society to improve it; his creatives ideas, although not as yet fully developed, could not relate to the social order of these new writers. His conception of society was one which included all of civilization; and his vision of the writer called for the totally involved moralist preaching a new order which must in no way be limited by a cool detachment. Even before he began his career as a serious writer, Wedekind permanently rejected Naturalism in favor of a freer, non-regulated form of expression.

However, developments at home changed the focus of Wedekind's literary interests. Late in the fall of 1886, the increasing tension caused by Frank's obvious disaffection with his law studies reached a danger point. Returning home, he was involved in a bitter argument with his father concerning his future, during which the bitter old man violently accused his wife of encouraging Frank's disobedience. Frank lost his temper and in a rage attacked his father. As Kutscher states it, "With one blow his entire life had been changed."[7]

The blessings which resulted from this family uproar were distinctly mixed. Wedekind was now free to dedicate himself to his writing, for he was banished from his home and made responsible only to himself. His most immediate problem was that of financial support. His lack of resources prohibited a return to school, since he actually did not have enough funds for daily sustenance. At this moment Karl Henckell once again interceded and arranged an interview with the internationally known Maggi Corporation, the world's largest manufacturer of boullion cubes. A few weeks after the family quarrel Wedekind was appointed chief of the advertising bureau for Maggi and settled down to work in Zurich, independent and in a state of considerable excitement.

But he soon tired of singing the praises of Herr Maggi's ubiquitous pellets. After barely six months Wedekind resigned and began freelancing for the Zurich newspapers, most notably for the *Neue Zürcher Zeitung*. In one of these articles, published in two parts, he considered for the first time a subject which was to fascinate him throughout his entire life: the circus. In "Zirkusgedanken," published in 1887, he explored the esthetics of motion in relation to circus performers and animals. In these pages, he develops a morality of physical perfection apart from social standards of action and explores a theme which was to become the foundation of his later writings: "The body has its own morality." Wedekind suggests that in the spiritual and physical equilibrium of the circus one might find the perfect balance of "Geist und Körper," intellect and body. In a sense he considers the circus from the intellectual perspective found in the painters of a later generation, when artists such as Picasso, Beckmann, and Rouault once again singled out the circus for special attention.

Meanwhile, Wedekind had completed two full-length plays, which represented his first serious attempts at dramatic writing. *Der Schnellmaler oder Kunst und Mammon* and *Elins Erweckung*, the latter written partly in collaboration with Henckell. But the full focus of his attention remained splintered, because he could not reconcile himself to the break with his father. After a year, during which the two men neither saw nor heard from one another, Frank wrote to his father and was rebuffed. In a state of depression, he wrote his mother and suggested that perhaps the only solution would be his removing himself permanently to America: "Europe is, if you permit me to say so, repugnant to me."[8] In Lenzburg the family urged Dr. Wedekind to forget the differences with his son. Finally, the father relented and telegraphed Frank to return home. Frank's reply, which barely arrived before he did, suggests to what extent the family strife had affected him: "I have acted in a way which has made me the most miserable of human beings."[9] Once again Frank was admitted into the family, but the matter was not to end there. Like Kafka, Wedekind's relations with his father were to have private as well as public repercussions and remained part of his spiritual and literary background as long as he lived.

### III  *Wedekind and Gerhart Hauptmann*

In a highly dramatic fashion, Wedekind's family troubles became the center of one of the most monumental literary feuds in German intellectual history, that between Wedekind and Gerhart Haupt-mann.[10]

Having settled with his father, Frank kept his apartment in Zurich, which was fast becoming one of the literary hotbeds of Europe. A band of expatriate German writers, refugees from political censor-ship at home, gathered there and organized a club, *Das junge Deutschland*. Carl and Gerhart Hauptmann, Henckell, and the an-archist John Henry Mackay formed the nucleus of the group, and Henckell once again attempted to bring Wedekind into the fold of the Naturalists. These young writers would sit together nightly, dis-cussing the latest innovations in literature and reading the theoretical works of Zola, the Hart brothers, and Conradi. But as in Munich Wedekind felt totally out of sympathy with their artistic ideas. His spiritual alienation from Naturalism was intensified by Wedekind's association with Gerhart Hauptmann, in whom he discovered his antithesis. To him Hauptmann was no more than a detective gather-ing facts in a notebook, "who then promptly every fall travels to Berlin with a milieu drama in his pocket."[11] Many years later, still intrigued by the contrast between himself and Hauptmann, Wede-kind tabulated what he considered the polarity. The left-hand col-umn reflects Wedekind's image of himself:

| | |
|---|---|
| egoist | altruist |
| night creature | day creature |
| thinker | artist |
| clumsy | creative |
| Peer Gynt | Brand |
| Franz Moor | Karl Moor |
| Mephisto | Faust |
| pessimist | optimist |
| theoretician | original thinker |
| gains by fighting | ethical, makes a grand career out of playing the "grand seigneur" |
| self-conscious | selfless, preaches universal love, compassion, understanding |
| genuine, but ugly | charming, but not genuine, artifi-ciality disfigures everything, joy in the beauty of the empty word |

When Wedekind made these observations, Hauptmann had already gained recognition as Germany's major dramatist, while Wedekind was still struggling for a reputation not simply based on notoriety. The bitterness, however, is a holdover from their early contact in

Zurich. During several of these evening sessions, Wedekind, in great detail, related to his friends the events of his family life which had led to the friction with his father. Unknown to him, Hauptmann was keeping a notebook of these incidents, which later served as the material for his family tragedy *Das Friedensfest.* It was an impropriety that Wedekind never forgave, and the resulting rupture between the two writers was never healed. Wedekind repaid Hauptmann in part by satirizing him mercilessly in *Die junge Welt,* his next play.

Then, with a suddenness which had always marked the intrusion of family matters into Wedekind's life, his father died on October 11, 1888, and once again he was forced to give up his literary apprenticeship.

## IV

*"When I last saw him, he looked like a young Faust, with his full, flaming beard, his eyes hungry for happiness beneath a brow that threatened fate itself; but now he is Mephistopheles, with his goatee and eyes that avert one's glance."*

Olga Plümacher, Christmas 1891

Wedekind was now genuinely free. With the death of his father, the family unit disintegrated. Mrs. Wedekind soon began to negotiate the sale of Schloss Lenzburg, and with the liberal inheritance money each of the children went his own way. Zurich and Lenzburg no longer served as magnets constantly attracting Frank home, and as soon as the estate was settled, he left for Berlin, to find, as he had hoped, the mainstream of European intellectualism.

Instead he found the Naturalists firmly entrenched and Gerhart Hauptmann recognized as the leading writer of the movement. Once again efforts were made to convert Wedekind to the tenets of Naturalism. While accepting the sociability of Julius and Heinrich Hart, he continued to argue for a freer mode of expression. Above all he could not abide the "Tendenz" of Naturalistic literature, the attacks which were made in the name of social justice against the middle-class morality which, in Wedekind's eyes, did no more than impose still another morality no less stultifying and smothering than that which it wanted to replace. Although he personally was committed to causes which underlined the insipidness of bourgeois morality, Wedekind rejected the use of art in their behalf. He argued with his friends in favor of an inner reality which did not necessarily reflect the image of life as it existed. He found the language of Naturalism above all boring, non-poetic, and drab. As had happened in Munich and Zurich, this confrontation between Wedekind and the leaders of the Naturalistic movement ended in a stalemate. Indeed, it is surprising to what extent Wedekind remained personally close to these writers throughout his literary career, in spite of his often outspoken rejection of their theories.

Wedekind's stay in Berlin was interrupted by the intervention of the police, who were not satisfied with his identification papers professing his American citizenship. They insisted on a passport verifying Wedekind's claims, and when he was unable to produce one, he was forced to leave. In July, 1889, he arrived in Munich, re-established his friendship with Michael Georg Conrad and actually became a member of the *Gesellschaft für modernes Leben,* the Munich-based organization dedicated to the propagation of Naturalism. But he could no longer find sufficient interest in this constant "clubbing" with like-minded people and dedicated himself to finding meaningful friendship outside of the Naturalist circle. He found one such person in Hans Richard Weinhöppel, a composer and musician who was to remain one of Wedekind's most loyal friends, a source of stability and ever ready help.

But by far the most important association of this period was his meeting with one of the great eccentric Bohemian personalities of Europe, Willi Morgenstern, known professionally as W. W. Rudinoff. He was, in every sense, an extraordinary individual. The son of a Polish-Jewish cantor, Rudinoff began his career as a teen-aged bit-player in Berlin theaters, but soon gravitated to the circus, where he became one of Europe's most distinguished clowns. Yet he loved the intimacy of the cabaret and was in great demand as a performer in an almost bewildering variety of entertainments. He gained fame as a bird imitator, whistler, silhouettist, singer, and artist. He sketched patrons in burnt cork and water color and achieved sufficient recognition as a painter, for his works to be exhibited in art galleries in Dresden, Berlin, Munich, and Vienna. His vocal talents led him to train as an operatic singer under Enrico Caruso's teacher, and eventually he sang several roles in the Viennese opera. A man of astounding energy, Rudinoff added to his larger-than-life image by being also an eccentric. He was a compulsive traveler, and his sudden appearance in the most improbable corners of the world, from the Caucasus to the Australian bush country, made headlines.

Wedekind was most attracted by Rudinoff's antic nature. He

would accompany him to various waterfront bars, where Rudinoff, in black-face, would impersonate African sailors. Rudinoff introduced his young friend into the "Schwabing" society of Munich's most notorious section, an often cacophonous mixture of nightclubs, bordellos, and dens. Through Rudinoff, Wedekind added to his experience what Robert Brustein calls "the underside of life." To his intellectual arsenal Wedekind now added all forms of popular entertainment, variety theater, pantomime, and songs of the back alley. It was the interaction of the literary tradition with the non-literary demimonde which created the uniquely Wedekindian image of life.

This first Munich phase proved to be a very productive one for Wedekind. He began work on another play immediately after completing *Die junge Welt*. By Easter of 1891, he had finished the work which eventually was to be recognized as one of his most durable plays: *Frühlings Erwachen*. His activity, however, had no bearing on his reputation. With *Der Schnellmaler* and *Die junge Welt*—originally published as *Kinder und Narren*—already in print, along with some verse and newspaper articles, Wedekind was still completely unknown to the public. When *Frühlings Erwachen* appeared in Zurich late in 1891 (the cost of publication was paid by the author himself), the play received no critical attention. Thanks to his biting attack on the Naturalists and Hauptmann in *Die junge Welt*, there was no hope of a stage production in any of the literary centers of Europe. Disappointed, in search of a new environment, Wedekind left Munich for Paris, arriving in December, 1891, at twenty-seven as an unknown writer suffering a self-imposed exile.

## V  *Paris and London*

Through Rudinoff's connections, Wedekind spent most of the next two years backstage in Parisian circuses, hobnobbing with a variety of clowns, weight-lifters, and bareback riders. His friends, with few exceptions, were German or Swiss writers who had flocked to Paris to escape the stifling intellectual atmosphere of Germany. Weinhöppel was a constant companion before he left for New Orleans with a touring French opera company in 1892. That December Rudinoff arrived in Paris, so Wedekind once again enjoyed the company of his boon companion.

Perhaps the most unusual relationship of this Paris visit was that which grew between Wedekind and the widow of the *Jung Deutschland* poet of the mid-nineteenth century, George Herwegh. Emma Herwegh was seventy-six years old and lived in fashionable poverty in Paris, where she found her happiest hours in relating stories about her husband to anyone who would take the time to listen. Wedekind met her in 1892 and remained her close friend and collaborator until her death. He became involved in the edition of her husband's works and letters and served as her representative to various publishers in Germany.

Wedekind's energy, in spite of his affection for Paris, kept him on the move. Twice he returned to Switzerland to visit friends, and in January, 1894, he left Paris for London, taking an apartment on Piccadilly Circus. In spite of the excitement of London night life, Wedekind, like Heine before him, liked neither England nor the English, whose company he made very little effort to cultivate. There has always been the inclination of expatriate writers to band together for security, as if they hoped to cut themselves off from the foreign environment of their temporary home. The "Young Germans" of Heine's generation in Paris, Brecht in California, and Wedekind in England demonstrated this self-enforced isolation. While in England Wedekind frequented only his countrymen. Armed with a letter of introduction, he contacted the daughter of Ferdinand Freiligrath, a friend and fellow poet who, with Herwegh, had formed the phalanx of the political poets of the previous generation. He also met the German writer Max Dauthendey, an acquaintance from Munich and one of the first German Symbolists. But Wedekind was no more receptive to his theories than he had been to Hauptmann's and soon fled.

His financial situation added to his distaste for England. In Munich and Paris he had raced through his inheritance and had been forced to turn to Mrs. Herwegh for assistance. His published works brought Wedekind no income, and while in London he was literally uncertain of his next meal. Fortunately, aid was forthcoming in the person of still another German literary figure, Otto Julius Bierbaum, whom Wedekind's friend Otto Erich Hartleben had told of his hardship. Hartleben also arranged for Wedekind to write a number of articles for German newspapers; and when he left London in August, 1894, Wedekind was rather impoverished.

Back in Paris, he was greeted by old friends while making new associations. Most important was his introduction to Lou Andreas-Salomé, friend of Nietzsche, Freud, and Rilke, and one of the most extraordinary women of her generation. Through her Wedekind reenforced his knowledge of Nietzsche and particularly Ibsen. He crystallized his own image of women by contrasting it to that which

Andreas-Salomé expounded in her book *Ibsens Frauengestalten,* published in 1892. In her circle of friends, Wedekind also met August Strindberg, who was living in Paris with his second wife, Frieda. His friendship with Strindberg was intense and brief; and by December of that year, after less than six months of very close contact, the two men broke with each other.

The Strindberg-Wedekind relationship was personal as well as intellectual. The visionary Swedish writer constituted in himself a theater in revolt. Much like Wedekind, he very early abandoned Naturalism to create a dramatic idiom which, in its technically innovative development, can easily be linked to Wedekind's. Both men wrestled simultaneously with the problem of Eros in modern civilization; and it has become an accepted cliché of dramatic criticism to consider Strindberg and Wedekind as the two "sex-directed" writers of their age. But their orientation and attitude toward the sexual force in mankind and the role of the female are in no way similar, and more than likely created a tension which played a significant role in the disintegration of their friendship. To Strindberg, the female represented the reincarnation of all that was evil and destructive in mankind; to Wedekind, as will be shown later, she was the embodiment of man's genuine inner needs, the expression of a beautiful instinct. No doubt this fundamental difference in their thinking regarding women had something to do with Frieda Strindberg's divorce several years later, after which she left for Munich, to live with Wedekind and bear him a child.

Still another contributor to Wedekind's "education" in Paris was an individual with the dubious distinction of being one of Europe's greatest art forgers. Wedekind became the personal secretary of Willi Gretor, a Dane whose "renderings" of Michelangelo, Leonardo da Vinci, and Andrea della Robbia are still apt to emerge in various locations in Europe and Africa, where they had been judiciously planted by Gretor and his associates over half a century ago.

Wedekind's Paris-London sojourn was particularly productive from the point of literary activity. He completed several major plays —*Der Liebestrank, Erdgeist,* and *Das Sonnenspektrum*—four ballet-pantomime pieces, and a great deal of poetry. He had also found in Albert Langen a publisher who was willing to give his works a maximum of exposure. When Wedekind left for Berlin in 1895, he entertained hopes of having his *Erdgeist* accepted by *Die Freie Bühne,* one of the leading avant-garde repertory companies of Germany, the company which had presented the German premieres of Ibsen's

*Ghosts* and Gerhart Hauptmann's *Vor Sonnenaufgang*. But to Wedekind's great disappointment the play was rejected, and he returned
to Munich in a state of great depression. His friends urged him to
abandon the anti-Naturalistic style he had adopted in his plays, but
Wedekind persisted. He took his plays to anyone who would listen
to a reading: the Harts, Max Halbe, Otto Brahm, who was the
director of the Deutsches Theater, and even to Gerhart Hauptmann,
an act which must have pained Wedekind greatly. The humiliation
of having to face the now famous Hauptmann, begging for the
chance of having his plays performed, and then meeting with refusal,
represents the low point of Wedekind's self-esteem.

Everywhere he took his work he was met with perplexity. The
small groups of listeners which Wedekind managed to cajole into
attending a reading found his plays confused, irrational, and totally
out of touch with reality. It was no wonder that Wedekind earnestly
considered abandoning his career as a writer, when the Munich-
based publisher Langen contacted him in the summer of 1895 with
the proposition that Wedekind join him in the founding of a new
magazine. Langen wanted Wedekind to serve as a senior editor and
contributor for a new kind of journal which would be distinguished
by satire, criticism of Philistinism, and a distinctly anti-royalist posture. The main target was to be the general tone of life in Wilhelmian
Germany. Wedekind had little reason to refuse, and he played a
major role in the organization of what was to become Germany's
outstanding contribution in the field of popular journalism, *Simplizissimus*.

That *Simplizissimus* was an instant success was in no small part
due to one of the most illustrious group of contributors in journalis-
tic history. Knut Hamsun, Rilke, both Heinrich and Thomas Mann,
Marcel Prevost, Hugo von Hofmannsthal, Detlev von Liliencron,
Arthur Schnitzler, Wilhelm Schaefer, Jakob Wassermann, and writers
of similar stature were more or less staff members, while some of
Germany's leading artists served as illustrators. With *Simplizissimus*
Langen offered the German public a magazine in the best tradition
of the anti-establishment literary organ.

Wedekind was the single most active contributor in the first few
years of publication. His stories, articles, interviews, and countless
cartoon captions gave him an exposure to the public which he had
never had until then. His biting wit gave the magazine its character
and tone, and more than any other of the "regulars," Wedekind's
name was associated with *Simplizissimus*. But other than stabilizing

his financial situation, the recognition caused him little satisfaction: "I want to be taken for a serious writer, and they recognize me as a clown." With four plays published, along with a volume of short stories, Wedekind's reputation rested on his notoriety as a sniping critic and social commentator for a satirical magazine. This image of the artist unable to find an audience was beginning to disturb Wedekind to such an extent that it became the major theme of his next play, *Der Kammersänger,* as well as of a whole range of plays written during the next decade of struggle for a fame which extended, hopefully, beyond notoriety. There was, as the critic Kurt Martens has pointed out, "something of the whipped dog about him."[12] As the decade of the 1890's was drawing to a close, Wedekind had yet to see one of his plays performed. His career was going nowhere, and his personal life was tinged with misfortune. The brief love affair with Frieda Strindberg, which had begun in the summer of 1896, came to a close the following year, but not before she gave birth to a son, on August 18, 1897. It was necessary for Wedekind to assume the responsibility of support for the child, and he gave up his futile search for a producer to return to the staff of *Simplizissimus.*

## VI  *Recognition—and Prison*

The magazine's publisher, Albert Langen, determined editorial policy and felt that in spite of the growing audience there was need for additional bite. Wedekind was asked to write a series of political poems attacking the government, but when his satirical knife proved too much for the censors, the issues in which these poems appeared were either banned or confiscated. The publicity was welcomed by Langen, and with the sale of available copies zooming, he urged Wedekind on, assuring him that since none of these poems appeared over Wedekind's name, there was no personal danger for their author. Dutifully, Wedekind handed over a last batch to the enterprising publisher. He had more important things to consider, for to his own astonishment he had found an interested producer.

Kurt Martens, long an admirer of Wedekind and leader of the *Leipziger Literarische Gesellschaft,* has contacted the dramatist about a possible production of *Erdgeist.* Wedekind was, of course, ecstatic and left Munich immediately for Leipzig, where on February 25, 1898, in the Kristallpalast a Wedekind play appeared on stage for the first time anywhere, under the direction of the noted German theater figure Carl Heine.

The production of *Erdgeist* was a success. After the premiere,

Heine took the company on a brief tour, and Wedekind's play was seen in Halle, Hamburg, and Breslau, returning to Leipzig to complete a ten-day run. But as monumental—or even more significant if that is possible—an event as Wedekind's debut as a dramatist was his debut as an actor! After searching for weeks for a suitable actor to play the difficult role of Dr. Schön, Heine suggested that Wedekind himself try reading the part. Wedekind, who was as scornful of Naturalistic acting as he was of the Naturalistic theater, gave an astonishing performance which, although puzzling Heine and the rest of the company, thoroughly polarized the main characters of the play. Deliberately abandoning the accepted "Stanislavskian" style which the Russian director had made famous at the Moscow Art Theatre in his interpretations of Chekhov, Wedekind introduced a highly stylized mode of acting, devoid of any psychological consistency. He was outrageously wooden in his movements, grotesquely exaggerated in his speech, and, while mystifying the respectable audiences who saw the performance, somehow gave a cohesiveness to the play which was missing when it was performed in a more "traditional" style. When because of illness he was replaced for the Hamburg performance, the play was interrupted by hooting from the audience, which developed into a full-fledged riot, forcing Heine to cancel the scheduled performance in Stettin.

With this sudden breakthrough Wedekind's prospects were definitely improving. Late in the summer of 1892, J. G. Stollberg, director of the Munich *Schauspielhaus*, called Wedekind to offer him a regular position as critic and—to Wedekind's surprise—actor. On October 29th, Stollberg produced *Erdgeist*, again with Wedekind in the male lead. Wedekind was now launched on two careers in the theater and was gaining the momentum which, he hoped, would lead to the performance of his other plays, when he was caught up in a bizarre affair involving Langen and *Simplizissimus,* and once again calling attention away from the serious dramatist to the notorious scandalizer.

Wedekind's relations with his publisher had never been satisfactory. Wedekind sensed that there was something of the exploiter in Langen, who always underpaid his staff while urging them on to greater accomplishments. As has been mentioned, it was under Langen's guarantee of protection that Wedekind undertook the writing of the anti-government poems, although he was all too willing to attack the emperor, German militarism, imperialism and publicly to express his own commitment to pacifism.[13] Among the verse

Wedekind had given to Langen was one which ridiculed the Kaiser's recent trip to Palestine. The censor had told Langen not to publish it, but it appeared nonetheless anonymously in *Simplizissimus,* and a warrant was issued for the arrest of the publisher and author. Langen fled to Switzerland, and when the police searched his office, they discovered Wedekind's manuscript copy of the poem, which revealed him as the author. Wedekind was charged with "Majestäts-beleidigung," libeling the crown. Although he was still under the employ of Stollberg in Munich, Wedekind had the choice of remaining in Germany to face arrest or leaving the country. Taking the advice of his friends, he left for Zurich and a bitter confrontation with Langen.

Cut off from his income and miserable away from Munich, Wedekind, for more than a year, wandered aimlessly through Europe before returning to Germany in June, 1899. The trial caused a sensation, with the liberal faction defending him in the face of governmental intervention with a free press. "The Wedekind Case" was debated on front pages all over Europe long after he was convicted on August 3. On September 22 he was brought to Königstein Prison, outside of Dresden. Wedekind was, to be sure, a celebrity, but hardly with the reputation he wanted. The government's case also focused attention on the "scurrilous" nature of his plays, which were attacked as immoral and undermining the ethics of the *Reich.* All sorts of religious organizations defended the government's action and branded Wedekind as a social outcast, although the circulation of *Erdgeist* and what was considered his other objectionable piece, *Frühlings Erwachen,* could hardly have warranted such attacks. Wedekind was attacked, but still not read.

In prison Wedekind used his time to complete still another play, *Der Marquis von Keith,* and his first longer prose work, *Mine-Haha.* He was released on March 3, 1900, after serving almost six months. He returned to a minor hero's welcome in Munich, greeted by friends and civil libertarians of all persuasions. He was invited to join the *Akademisch-dramatischer Verein,* whose membership included the leading intellectuals of Munich. Wedekind attained the stature of a symbolic figure for the avant-garde and anti-establishment factions in Germany, who demonstrated much interest in his martyrdom, but little in his literary works. However, the notoriety of the trial and imprisonment caused a rippling of interest on the part of the theatrical world, and *Der Kammersänger,* which had been premiered in Berlin during his incarceration, was performed in several theaters in various parts of Germany. The advance which he received for *Der Marquis von Keith* from the Insel-Verlag—he no longer had anything to do with Langen—provided him with pocket money.

## VII   *Das Überbrettl*

Still, these were insufficient funds for him to support himself and his shadow family, Frieda Strindberg and her son Friedrich. Wedekine found another source of income in the Munich night life and its offbeat inhabitants.

"Das Überbrettl," the small, intimate cabaret-theater, was flourishing in Germany. Several of these operated with great success in the freer intellectual climates of Berlin, Hamburg, and Munich. In April, 1901, a Frenchman, Georges d'Ailly-Vaucheret, opened *Die elf Scharfrichter* in Munich. It was only natural that he would turn to Wedekind as a prime attraction for his club. The latter's reputation as a gad-fly, the sensationalism of his trial, and his association with all elements of the intellectual community as well as the Bohemian world, made Wedekind a celebrity and provided d'Ailly-Vaucheret with a ready-made drawing card. Wedekind, who had taught himself guitar and lute, possessed, as Brecht notes in the obituary, a coarse but powerful voice. He put together a night-club act which kept him as premiere performer with top billing at *Die elf Scharfrichter*, where he performed nightly until the end of July. The act consisted primarily of Wedekind's singing his own songs, generally with melodies of his own invention. For his material he revived the art of the street-singer, delighting his audiences with songs of murder, lust, and sad prostitutes. He became, in effect, Germany's outstanding "Bänkelsänger" in his own time. His impact on the cabaret stage was striking. Wedekind created a new style of singing with his brittle, cutting voice, relying on the "Zungen-R" effect to create this harshness, which matched the brutality of the lyrics. Anyone who has seen or heard the street-singer at the beginning of Brecht's *Die Dreigroschenoper*, written in 1929, as he nasally intones the vices of Macheath in the "Moritat von Mackie Messer," must sense the impact of Wedekind's style.

## VIII   *Success and Censorship*

But once again this was not the fame that Wedekind wanted. He continued to write, completing *König Nicolo, oder So ist das Leben* in 1902. In this work, Wedekind clearly expresses the bitterness which he felt in his life. His vision of himself was that of a tragic clown, misunderstood, ridiculed, and abused by a cruel public. In *König Nicolo* he chronicles the life of an exiled king who reappears at his former court in the role of a jester, dying amidst the laughter of the court while the true nobility of his birth goes undetected.

But the self-pity of *König Nicolo* and several of the plays which followed was really uncalled for. The relative success of *Der Kammersänger* won him some critical acclaim, and reviewers as well as producers turned to the earlier plays for belated consideration. Fortunately for Wedekind, he had some notable supporters, particularly Alfred Kerr and Karl Kraus, who were among the earliest "discoverers." But the most decisive factor in Wedekind's favor was the decision of Max Reinhardt to produce *Erdgeist* at the *Kleines Theater* in Berlin. Reinhardt had served his theatrical apprenticeship under Otto Brahm at the *Deutsches Theater*, but in 1902 he set out on his own. An innovator in every respect, he saw in Wedekind's *Erdgeist* a vehicle with which he could challenge the supremacy of the Naturalists, and when the play opened on December 17, 1902, both Reinhardt and Wedekind entered a new phase of their lives. Reinhardt was to go on to become the outstanding theatrical figure of his generation; and thanks to his efforts, Wedekind, almost overnight, became a literary celebrity, independent of his reputation as a questionable character. During the season of 1903–4, there were 149 performances of his plays in Germany. He was heralded as having slain the dragon of Naturalism by giving the German theater a completely new sense of dramatic values. Albert Langen and Wedekind settled their differences, and the publisher brought out new editions of the plays. The critics filled newspapers all over Germany with reviews of Wedekind's plays. George Brandes, Paul Lindau, Richard Dehmel, among the leading writers of the first decade of the new century, followed the lead of Kerr and Kraus in suggesting that Wedekind had created a new theater for Europe. The critic Friedrich Kayssler summed up this sentiment when reviewing *Erdgeist*: "Do you realize what you have done today? You have strangled the naturalistic monster called 'probability' and returned the element of play to the stage. Long may you live!"[14]

The recognition had come. Along with frequent performances of his plays, Wedekind was in great demand as an actor and spent much of the theatrical season as guest performer in his own plays as well as in the entire repertory. In October, 1903 the first Wedekind cycle was staged, in Nürnberg's *Intimes Theater*, to be followed by several others within the next two years.

But Wedekind's increasing popularity and literary reputation also served another purpose, that of unifying those forces which had been opposed to him, but which never took him as a serious threat. Since his *Simplizissimus* days, Wedekind had been obnoxious to the government, but now private organizations and individual citizens took it upon themselves to attack him and his works as reflecting moral depravity. The heroine of *Erdgeist*, Lulu, his ideal of "Das Ewig-Weibliche" and the embodiment of the female sex drive which devastates the middle-class society around it, was criticized as the product of a degenerate mind. It seemed, as the literary historian Günter Seehaus points out, that the anti-Wedekind forces in Germany organized themselves only after his works began to be popular after 1900.[15]

It was the government which took the lead in attacking Wedekind. With the publication of the sequel to *Erdgeist*, *Die Büchse der Pandora* (1905), the full power of the censor was put into motion. Public performance was forbidden, and while the play was staged in Vienna, it was not performed in Germany until after the abolition of the censor in 1918. Charges of obscenity were officially made, and Wedekind and his publisher Bruno Cassirer were brought to trial. Once again Wedekind found himself in court, but this time with the full support of liberal groups from all over Europe. The *Schutzverband deutscher Schriftsteller* fought the case through the law courts of Leipzig and Berlin, and although the ban remained in effect, the affair united German intellectuals behind Wedekind and gave him an increased exposure to the public. He was, as Seehaus states, "a symbol in the struggle for freedom of the intellect against the anachronistic domination of the authorities."[16] From this point to the end of his life, Wedekind's name was inevitably tied to governmental censorship. His friends called for the formation of a "Wedekind-Bund" in 1911 to assist other writers who were in conflict with the censor. By this time almost all of his plays, regardless of their themes, had been placed under some restriction by the government.

Beginning with Reinhardt's production of *Frühlings Erwachen*, which was given its initial staging in Berlin in 1905 and ran for an astonishing 321 performances, Wedekind grew to one of the most conspicuous dramatists in Germany. With the allegiance of some of Europe's most astute individuals, even some of the stigma of his reputation began to wear off. Walter Rathenau and Thomas Mann called him one of the foremost moralists of the Continent and a dramatic innovator of the first rank. Wedekind needed all the respectability he could muster. Although his personal life seemed to settle down with his marriage to the actress Tilly Newes in May, 1906, he still managed to scandalize the popular press and the guardians of public morality.

The newspapers in general vilified him and his plays, while exploiting his earlier Bohemianism, now that he was worth attacking. The *Allgemeine Rundschau* led the onslaught against Wedekind's "foul-smelling plays," while newspapers with church affiliations condemned him as a destroyer of national morality. The criticism was indiscriminately flung at the works and their author, and a Wedekind image began gradually to emerge from the wave of publicity. Even to those who never read his plays, Wedekind was "news": his name was connected with the exotic and erotic, with perversion and pornography, and to the sensational yellow press he was made to appear the embodiment and reincarnation of the Marquis de Sade! This was the myth created by the press: Wedekind the arch-pornographer, banned by the censor, attacked by the church, a destroyer of human values.

Besides individuals like Mann and Rathenau most German literary journals gave Wedekind their unstinting support. *Pan, Die Aktion,* and *Der Sturm* editorialized in favor of Wedekind's works and character; and abroad he was receiving more acclaim (and productions) than most of his countrymen, including Hauptmann.[17] Wedekind, in his forties, was to a vocal segment of the literate world an established and upright writer. His marriage to Tilly was a happy one, and with the arrival of children he assumed these responsibilities willingly and with great dedication.[18] Yet the battle of Wedekind factions, which had been raging for more than a decade in the press and public, now moved to the academic halls, and sufficient honor was bestowed on him to bring an additional measure of respectability. In September, 1912, he was invited as an honored guest to the matriculation ceremonies at the University of Dublin; and the year before he presented a speech on Heinrich von Kleist to a gathering of distinguished scholars gathered at the Munich *Schauspielhaus.* Through his friend Kutscher, Wedekind was given permission to address the theater classes at the university in Munich and often led informal discussions. But Kutscher's first all-university lecture on Wedekind caused an uproar among the faculty, and the rector informed him that Wedekind's name would not be permitted to appear in the catalogue! The effect of his Wedekind studies on Kutscher's career has already been noted.

## IX  *The Last Years*

The final decade of Wedekind's life before his death in 1918 saw him established, yet insecure. His major dramatic works were behind him, but he continued to produce plays at the rate of almost one a year: *Hidalla, oder Karl Hetmann der Zwergriese* (1903), *Totentanz* 1905), *Musik* (1906), *Die Zensur* (1907), *Oaha, die Satire der Satire* (1908), *Schloss Wetterstein* (1910), *Franziska* (1911), *Simson* (1914), *Bismarck* (1916), and *Herakles* (1917). He spent this last decade admired by the intellectuals, haunted by the censor, sensationalized in the popular press, and viewed with a prurient curiosity by the public. Besides his dramatic works, Wedekind poured out dozens of pamphlets, essays, and speeches, most of them in an effort to establish the validity of his moral position in matters of sex, politics, militarism, acting, and countless other topics.

In "Über Erotik," which served as a foreword to the collected short stories published by Georg Müller in 1910, Wedekind publicly defended his sexual code. The fundamental distinction which remains muddled in the minds of most people, pleads Wedekind, is that between obscenity and the honest effort to make man's basic sexual instinct comprehensible. He lashes out against the real purveyors of obscenity, those who make no effort to understand and who attempt to hide behind a cloak of moral indignation the deformities of a sick mind: "What is an obscenity? It is a mockery, a debasement, an insult to sexuality. If sexual matters were discussed intelligently, there would be less rape and lust murders. . . . Obscenity is to true sexuality what cursing is to religion." (I, 205)[19] He repeats the plea for enlightenment in matters of sexual education in "Aufklärungen," offering his plays as excellent examples of an intellectual approach to matters of sex, and suggesting, as he always had, that society, in its instinctive urge to repressiveness in matters of sexuality, was betraying its fear of freedom.

Almost instinctively Wedekind embraced the minority opinion. In "Weltlage," written just before the outbreak of the First World War and at the height of German nationalism, he traces the growth of militaristic and nationalistic impulses in Europe and blames them for all the current tensions. Wedekind was a committed internationalist before the outbreak of the war, and in "Weihnachtsgedanken" he calls for the formation of a world parliament, a perpetual peace conference with operations constantly shifting between the major cities in the world, so that prestige and power might be equally divided.

Such pronouncements gave him greater respect in those circles which already honored him, and alienated him more from those that detested him. By his admirers Wedekind was revered as befitted a martyr to the cause of literary and intellectual integrity, which is how they viewed him. His friends took the occasion of his fiftieth birthday in 1914 to do him great honor, with the journal *Die Zukunft* setting off what was to be more or less "a Wedekind year" with an official appeal for the establishment of a "Wedekind Prize" in literature. The *Zukunft* article was signed by Herbert Eulenberg, Kurt Martens, and Thomas Mann, "to give to this poet, who, as one of our most significant dramatists, has had to battle and suffer for the freedom of expression even to this very day, a small measure of our esteem and especially a sign of public honor."[20] The magazine *Forum* published a lead editorial urging the German theater industry to single out Wedekind for special recognition during the entire year; and once again Thomas Mann acted as a sponsor. Almost every literary guild in Munich paid tribute to him at a variety of testimonial dinners.

The high point of the year's activities was the publication of the *Wedekindbuch*, a collection of essays edited by Joachim Friedenthal and written by Wedekind's most ardent admirers. The book reads like a "Who's Who" of German life and letters; contributors included Hermann Bahr, Richard Dehmel, Eulenberg, Bruno Frank, Max Halbe, Carl Hauptmann (his brother's name is conspicuously missing), Alfred Kerr, Kutscher, both Manns, Rathenau, Wilhelm von Scholz, Carl Sternheim, Jakob Wassermann, Stefan Zweig, and almost every major director and actor in Germany.

In the midst of the greatest tribute ever paid him, with his plays enjoying an incredible number of productions all over Germany and Europe, Wedekind's moment of glory came to an abrupt end with the outbreak of the war, one week after his birthday. All theaters were closed, including the Munich *Kammerspiele*, where an extensive Wedekind cycle was underway. When the theaters opened once again that fall, his works were almost totally absent. It was as if a grand conspiracy had been effected between the military and the censorship—which was, to be sure, in the hands of the military authorities. Wedekind's works were declared "undesirable" and, above all, bad for the morale of the troops! When theaters had the temerity to attempt a production, the newspapers and periodicals that supported the government inevitably took the same hard line. Reviewing *Der Marquis von Keith* in January, 1915, for the popular magazine

*Hochland,* the critic Karl Muth attacked Wedekind: "There is nothing to compare to the scandal of what was seen last evening, especially for anyone who has a sense of responsibility about our times,
our people, and especially about our warriors out in the battlefield."[21]
The patriotic protests against Wedekind continued throughout the
war years, so that it was almost impossible to bring out an edition
of any of his works. When the Georg Müller Verlag published a
modest paperback edition of *Frühlings Erwachen* as part of its
"Weltliteratur" series in 1918, a leading government official asserted
that this publication "represents a blow in the faces of our fighting,
wounded, and fallen heroes, a mockery of German aesthetics, against
which the state's judicial branch must act with determination."[22]
The attacks on his works and person reached a new pitch during
these war years. Even Wedekind's faithful supporters were silenced,
either by their own loyalty to the fatherland or by the nature of
Wedekind's own actions, which left many of his friends stunned and
shocked. For not long after the fighting had begun, he pledged his
allegiance to the cause of German victory.

It is impossible to say why Wedekind recanted. His intimate friend
Kutscher is unable to explain the sudden turnabout. Perhaps he was
growing weary of the constant battle with the censor and government. That he actually became convinced of the righteousness of the
German cause is unlikely, considering that until 1914 his pamphle-
teering clearly placed him in the camp of the liberal left. In any
case, Wedekind completely compromised his beliefs and principles.
As he told Kurt Martens, "One must run with the pack." On September 18, 1914, he took part in a "Fatherland Celebration" at the
*Kammerspiele,* making a speech which was later published as "Vom
deutschen Vaterlandsstolz" and "Deutschland bringt die Freiheit."
In these remarks, Wedekind makes a mockery of his international-
ism, his hatred of political intrigue, and what was a fundamental
distrust of diplomacy. He chronicles the history of Germany and
German unity, concluding that the war has brought the nation together as never before. In a German victory, he proudly boasts, lay
the hope for world peace: "There is no doubt that we Germans are
better prepared to handle the affairs of the French and Belgians to
their mutual benefit than they themselves are."[23]

The ultimate irony of Wedekind's completely unexpected chauvin-
ism was that it won him no support and affection in the eyes of the
public or government. The press continued to moralize against him,
and his last plays, which would seem hardly objectionable, were

prohibited nonetheless. *Simson* is a wooden, biblical verse drama that could hardly be called inflammatory; yet it was banned. Wedekind even attempted to write what seemed to him a passionately patriotic play. In *Bismarck* he attempted a faithful documentary of Bismarck's rise to power during the 1860's, using historical manuscripts and Bismarck's letters and writings for much of his text. But the censor thought it inopportune to dramatize the German-Austrian conflict at a time when the two nations were allied, and once again a Wedekind play was banned from the stage.

Strangely, Wedekind's new allegiance had little effect on his prestige among those followers who had established him as a literary idol. When he died on March 9, 1918, a cry of anguish went up from both the intellectual and Bohemian elements in Germany, and his funeral, three days later, with crowds of elegantly dressed mourners mixing with the "beats" from Munich's Schwabing Quarter, was a tribute to this loyalty. Ernst Hoferichter was an eyewitness and describes the proceedings:

This sad event was as strange and grotesque as was the poet's entire life. The sensational and macabre attracted large throngs of the curious public who mingled with the saddened mourners. Yes, it was as if the dead man wanted to make a last effort to represent his works on this earth, not wanting to forget the circus atmosphere. As the procession began moving away from the chapel where the benediction was read, the sensation-seekers ran and skipped ahead to the grave, jumped over old and peaceful graves. In front of the open grave there was set up—for the first time ever in Munich—a "news of the week in review" camera from the movies. I still remember the words of Heinrich Mann, of Erich Mühsam, and of Friedenthal. At the end Max Halbe spoke with great emotion Wedekind's own words: "Hail to the fighter, immortality crowns!" And finally, as a kind of apotheosis, the writer Heinrich Lautensack tried to leap into the open grave, screaming, "Your most humble pupil embraces you!"[24]

Even in death Wedekind was not able to transcend the sense of tragicomedy which marked his entire life. He battled for a sense of serious identity which was impossible. As the opposition he took on all of society, striking at the nerve-endings of a civilization which wanted no part of his new morality. But the impact of his actions, beliefs, and physical presence on a generation of writers who viewed him as a symbol of intellectual martyrdom had a profound effect on German as well as on European literature for years to come. And it is to these aspects of this "deeply tormented man," as Thomas Mann called him, that we now turn.[25]

# CHAPTER 3

# *Idea and Technique: The Early Plays*

WEDEKIND was first and foremost a dramatist, although until 1886, when he was twenty-two years old, his most significant literary efforts were in verse and prose narrative. His great passion was the theater, and he found his first model in the German dramatist Georg Büchner, who died in 1837 at the age of twenty-four.[1] He had written three major plays during his lifetime: the massive historical drama of the French Revolution, *Dantons Tod;* a romantic comedy, *Leonce und Lena;* and *Woyzeck,* a brutally grotesque drama about the sufferings of a lower-depths creature who confronts an unfeeling world of dehumanized mankind. Through all of Büchner runs the bleak fatalism of a visionary playwright who sees society as depraved and incorrigible. Büchner also created a technical corollary to this philosophical nihilism by dislocating and disrupting the structure of his plays in a fashion which found its ultimate echo in the German Expressionists a hundred years later. Scene rushes in upon scene, phrase vies with phrase. Büchner drew from a linguistic heritage rooted in Shakespeare, the commedia dell' arte, and the gutter. Allied to this violent world of negation is a black humor which makes Büchner's few dramatic writings among the most grotesque in all of dramatic literature.[2]

From the very outset Büchner's dramatic inventiveness had a major influence on Wedekind's writings for the stage. The hilarious is never far from the universally serious. The concept was more important than the characterization, and as a result, characterization was often replaced by caricature. Actually, almost half of Wedekind's plays are labeled as comedies, and, like Anton Chekhov, he had the unique ability to create in his dramatic works a tragicomic sense that marks his plays as being beyond the normal pale of dramatic convention.

Wedekind's first serious effort at dramatic writing served as a prelude for what came later to be known as "the Wedekind style." *Der Schnellmaler oder Kunst und Mammon,* "a great tragicomic original farce in three acts," was written in 1886, and besides serving as an exercise in his exploration of technique, it gave Wedekind an opportunity to try out the ideas which would mature eventually in the later works. In the best tradition of the Viennese popular "Volksstück," Wedekind employs every trick of dramatic gamesmanship so well-known on the Austrian and German stage: disguises, eavesdropping, an endless flow of letters, farcical entrances and exits demonstrate that Wedekind knew the popular stage of his time, particularly the plays of the most often produced nineteenth-century Austrian dramatists Raimund and Nestroy. The hero is a poor young artist named Fridolin, who is driven by a Byronic "Weltschmerz" to thoughts of suicide. A hallucination draws him toward death. He loves Johanna, daughter of the factory owner Pankratius Knapp, but his conscience keeps him from her until he can support his beloved. Johanna's brother urges Fridolin to give up his art in favor of business, but the young, unknown painter still has hopes of gaining fame through his last work, "Prometheus Unbound," in which, unfortunately, nobody is interested. Meanwhile, father Knapp has taken a fancy to a chemist named Dr. Steiner, who in reality is a confidence man. The two conspire to get rid of the love-sick Fridolin, leaving the way clear for Steiner to marry Johanna. After one unsuccessful attempt at suicide, Fridolin manages to evade his companions and drinks a potion which he believes to be poison, only to discover, to his dismay, that someone had substituted sugar water. Finally, Steiner's crooked dealings are uncovered; he is arrested, after having swindled Knapp out of a fortune. His true identity is established: that of the notorious Italian Pandulpho Paravinini from Padua! Fridolin sells his painting to the Royal Art Academy, and father Knapp blesses the young lovers.

No doubt, *Der Schellmaler* is little more than a trivial situation comedy with distinctly farcical overtones, but one notices particular qualities and concepts which Wedekind never abandoned. Already at this stage, Wedekind demonstrates a thorough dislike for the "homo economicus," the business man whose primary instinct is the making of money.[3] The conspiracy of Knapp and Steiner against the innocent artist Fridolin expresses humorously what was to become the grim struggle for existence in the later Wedekindian universe: the predatory animal's instinctive drive to destroy beauty. Entrenched society is represented by the figure of "Das Raubtier" which is bent on controlling or eradicating "das schöne, wilde Tier," the symbol of unrepressed sensuality and beauty.

Even in this first dramatic work, with its traditional elements of folk burlesque, Wedekind's sense of the comic stands out as something quite distinctive. Fridolin's urge for self-destruction, for all its farcical qualities, still gives the entire play an aura of death, which is never far from the comic. In Act I, Johanna's brother and a philosophy Professor, Dr. Chrysostomus Grübelmeier, are arguing with Fridolin. The former wants him to join the firm as a salesman, while the academician urges the distraught artist to align himself with the organization over which he presides, "The International Society for Suicide." Grübelmeier's arguments prevail, but while Fridolin is trying to find some moment of tranquillity so that he can kill himself properly, he is constantly harassed by Grübelmeier's associates in death: a coffin-maker who wants to measure the candidate, a grave-digger in search of a site and, finally, a grotesque funeral director worthy of a place in Evelyn Waugh's *The Loved One*. The good humor of the work is constantly undercut by this proximity of death, and the reader suspects that Fridolin may ultimately succeed in his suicide attempts and plunge the story into some unexpected tragic sphere. But Wedekind is careful never to delineate his characters so well as to involve the audience with their actions. Even Fridolin, for all his innocence, is a parody of the "Storm and Stress" hero and, at times, a bizarre, youthfully bombastic King Lear—as when he appears on stage in Act II, scene five. The scene is set in a wood, and Fridolin, madly in love with Johanna, enters "without hat or coat. He is completely disheveled":

Salvation, Salvation! Through storm and savage state comes this bluster on fire-breathing jades, triumph of his cracking whip, of his hunting horns exultant coloraturas! His bright-green riding breeches shine through thorn and thicket like the early grow at the trump of doom! . . . (beating himself around the head) Fool that I am, madman, blind beggar, who placed his hopes on faithfulness! (VII, 52)

All this is accompanied by "a wild music, punctuated by the howling storm and thunder claps." When the satire bites, it is directed inevitably against the businessmen. But fundamentally Wedekind's humor in *Der Schnellmaler* is benign, and the caricatures are never really destructive. Furthermore, no consideration is given to the theme of sexuality. Thus it is convenient for those critics who would concentrate on the erotic aspects of Wedekind's art to dismiss this

work as a false start. Yet, clearly, *Der Schnellmaler* is the obvious
first step, when viewed in respect to all of Wedekind's subsequent
plays. Even the dialogue is singularly his own. He abandons any
sense of psychological motivation and verisimilitude and creates a
language and tension which, even for the 1880's, was strikingly his
own. The characters do not communicate with one another, talk past
each other, and in effect exist in total isolation from the action of
the play. The "Aneinander-Vorbeireden" technique, coupled with a
language which has no basis in reality, was to become the hallmark
of Wedekind's dialogue. Through these devices Wedekind retains
the responsibility for his characters and never permits them to develop along naturalistic lines. Behind the burlesque aspects of the
play one can see a more significant development for the later more
serious plays, when this style would create a sense of complete alienation. But even in *Der Schnellmaler* there are clear hints of things to
come.

## I  Enter "das Freudenmädchen"

*Elins Erweckung* (1887) is still another exploratory work, but
introduces those additional themes which concerned Wedekind, so
that, along with *Der Schnellmaler*, it represents a crucial phase of
his intellectual progress. Written in part with Henckell's assistance,
it is not only Wedekind's first effort at writing a verse drama, but
also his initial dramatic exploration of the nature of sexuality. The
approach is one which serves as a prelude to the children's tragedy
*Frühlings Erwachen,* and both are expressions of Wedekind's own
experiences of youth, "the maturity of a youth tormented by sex."[4]
Elin is a theological student preparing for his first sermon on Easter
Sunday. He is tormented by feelings which he cannot account for
morally. His earlier spiritual unity is challenged by what seems to
him to be a revelation of his own impurity, "the awareness of the
powers of hell" within his soul: the sexual urge. In a cemetery he
confesses his feelings to his friend Oscar, a detached and enlightened
young physician. Elin's dreams have been filled with "impurities,"
and Oscar attempts to assure him that what appears to Elin as obscenity is perfectly normal, and that the expression of these instinctive
drives is psychologically and physiologically desirable. He urges
Elin, however, to avoid marital entanglements, which in Oscar's
mind only further restrict the genuine expression of these natural
urges. Suddenly, from behind a tombstone an old beggar named
Schigolch emerges to support Oscar's argument and invites the

young men to meet his ward, an orphaned girl whom he had discovered wandering through the city streets and whom he has "educated" in the beauties of love. The friends leave the bizarre hustler,
and their conversation turns to Elin's sermon, which Oscar attacks
for its moral dishonesty. In the midst of this conversation, a young girl
races in front of them as she is being chased by an elegantly dressed
man brandishing a knife. The girl is Ella, Schigolch's daughter, who
is being harassed by a comically lecherous and debauched nobleman, Count Schweinitz.[5] Saved by the intervention of the two perplexed young men, Ella is a picture of the righteous and chaste
maiden which she obviously is not, as she confronts her attacker
triumphantly:

Ella (*raising herself toward Schweinitz*): You believe no doubt that because I earn my daily bread with my naked body you would be permitted
to treat me as your dog? I am as little your personal property as you are —
an image of virtue! (IX, 52)

Elin is quite touched by this "martyr of civilization," and awakens
to a new emotional experience. Now freed from the bonds of his reli-
giously motivated constraints, he senses within himself the need to
transcend the entire moral order of society and, joined with Ella, he
marches off to create a new race of man.

The verse is often lumbering, and Wedekind was obviously having
a good deal of fun in his mock-melodramatic scenes, so that on its
own merits, other than some good clowning, the play has little to
recommend itself. But in the over-all view of Wedekind's developing
ideas there is a great deal of significance. *Elins Erweckung* represents
his initial expression of the theme of sexual emancipation, of freeing
mankind from its traditional inhibitions which are, to a large extent,
a product of his Christian education. Elin himself is a Nietzschean
"Übermensch" who finally rejects the constrictive forces of society,
and especially Christianity, which have produced in him a guilt
based on a fundamental hatred of sex.

He acquires his new knowledge through the efforts of a proud
and strangely noble prostitute, whose own attitude toward her vocation is strikingly idealized. She refuses to become what society would
make of her, a debased and obscene object of a lust devoid of any
sensual beauty. Civilization—in this case represented by the deli-
ciously villainous Count Schweinitz—is bestial and unaware of the
spiritual focus of sex, which Elin and Ella ultimately bring about.

The count's name, with its obvious reference to a pig, is Wedekind's blunt way of making his point. "Das Freudenmädchen" was meant to be literally what her name suggests, "a joyous girl," not what Schweinitz would make of her, a beaten, humiliated animal, thoroughly domesticated and crawling at the feet of society.

Dramatically, Wedekind used the play to try out characters and scenes which became crucial in his first major play, *Frühlings Erwachen*, as well as in the "Lulu" plays. The graveyard conversation between Elin and Oscar, in which Elin expresses his uncertainty about his chosen vocation, becomes the pivotal scene of *Frühlings Erwachen*, where two similar young men, Melchoir and Moritz, while sitting in a graveyard in front of Moritz' tombstone (he has returned to convince his friend that suicide is the only solution to life), discuss Melchior's fate. Ella's development is twofold. In *Frühlings Erwachen* she appears as Ilse, the gay, uncomplicated, and emancipated schoolgirl who escapes the suffocating life of her friends to find complete contentment in the life of a "Freudenmädchen"; and ultimately Wedekind transforms her into the mythical force, which is Lulu in *Erdgeist* and *Die Büchse der Pandora;* the embodiment of sexuality.

Count Schweinitz is the prototype of a character who repeatedly emerges in Wedekind's dramatis personae as the counterweight to Lulu's life force. Wedekind very early sensed a link between the "homo economicus" and the fundamental antipathy to a free, unrestricted eroticism. Throughout his plays, he parades a long line of social, economic, and sexual predatory types, robber barons of sex and society, who demonstrate a lust for power both financial and physical. Dedicated to the accumulation of wealth, these men inevitably come into conflict with an either sexually or morally emancipated representative of Wedekind's "positive" forces and ruthlessly go about destroying all efforts to accomplish a transformation of mankind's ethics. These "Raubtiere" are the surrogates of the economically oriented, rational, and civilization-conditioned society which Wedekind persistently attacks, but which inevitably win out. These individuals are consistently power hungry, as in Schweinitz' case, and extend this insatiable lust for power to the physical sphere, a "body and soul" domination of others.

However, it was still another ethical question hinted at in *Elins Erweckung* that led Wedekind directly to his next play, a work which was the most mature and dramatically satisfying of his early period. In his discussions with Elin, Oscar persistently attacks the institution of marriage, conceived of by modern society as the greatest enemy of man's natural instincts. In the grand conspiracy of civilization to control these natural passions, the institution of marriage had, in Wedekind's mind, become the prime instrument, and it was this "problem" which he tackled in *Die junge Welt* (1889), while at the same time articulating his final break with the literary and social implications of German Naturalism.

## II   Die junge Welt

One of Wedekind's earliest critics, Paul Fechter, has called *Die junge Welt* (originally entitled *Kinder und Narren*) "a most splendid overture to the main work to come."[6] It represents a synthesis of idea and form, such as Wedekind tried out in his first two dramatic works, and can be considered his first really "complete" dramatic effort. For the first time, Wedekind had an ax to grind as well as the material with which to grind it. He admitted the essentially autobiographical nature of the play: "I had hit upon the idea of putting together the individuals from my circle of acquaintances with the contents of my intellectual horizon." The result is one of the most hard-hitting literary satires in German dramatic literature. Specifically, the play results from Gerhart Hauptmann's impropriety in using events from Wedekind's personal life, which he meticulously recorded in his notebooks and later used in his *das Friedensfest*. Wedekind was furious about this breach of confidence and determined to get even with Hauptmann. But he aimed at more than a personal diatribe against a writer whom he disliked; he conceived of an attack on the artistic principles which Hauptmann advocated. In *Die junge Welt* Wedekind launched a two-pronged assault: against the "Wirklichkeitsschilderung" of the Naturalist writers, that minute description of the most insignificant details in the effort to capture total reality; and, more fundamentally, against what Wedekind regarded as spurious efforts to attain women's emancipation.

The main target of this literary lampoon is quite clearly Hauptmann himself, who appears as the poet Meier, a pompous and arrogant writer who walks through life with a notebook in his hand, jotting down observations of people as they go about their daily work. His major literary work is a play, *Vor Hellwerden,* an obvious parody of Hauptmann's *Vor Sonnenaufgang.* This thoroughly foolish young man is honored as a genius by the avant-garde theater, but detested by his friends for having used events in their own lives in his play. While honored by the outside world, he is hated by his intimates: "Because you don't know life, you are exhausted right down to the last drop of your blood and out of necessity have fallen into realism for your inspiration. But realism is a pedantic governess, and because of it you have forgotten what people are all about."[7]

At the same time, Wedekind hammers away at the "Frauenbewegung," the activities of the feminists aimed at gaining equality in a man's world. Wedekind viewed the movement with great skepticism. For a man who considered the ultimate femininity of the female to be her greatest attribute, her primary reason for existence, any effort to deny this quality in favor of a masculine imitation was heretical. For Wedekind "das Weibliche" was that which, above all else, must be preserved and developed if the female mystique was to have an effect on society. To renege on the responsibility of maintaining this femininity, to wear pants, to subdue those female virtues which are fundamental to women alone, seemed utterly unnatural to Wedekind.

The comedy begins with a prelude in a Swiss girls' school, where six young ladies are being instructed in art history by one Professor Ilsebein, a fuzzy pedant who serves as the prototype for all of Wedekind's devastating attacks on educators. The girls are of various minds concerning life, marriage, and children; but on one thing they are agreed: their current education is useless. Anna militantly believes that women must preserve their integrity as long as possible in order to gain equality in this male-oriented world. But when Alma, another young feminist, urges the girls not to marry until equality is achieved, another protests: "What will become of our children, if they don't have any mothers?" (II, 16) At the end, the more strongly committed girls are determined to struggle for emancipation and full equality.

The actual play begins several years later, when the girls come together to visit Marguerite, who has married an assessor and is living a life of doll-house splendor: "We don't read at all. He says I should always go bathing and swimming. If there's anything I want, all I have to do is ask him." (II, 30) Some of the collected group feel that this is the ideal marriage; others, most notably Anna, are repelled by this shirking of responsibility. The result is that the happy "young marrieds" try to convince the unmarried girls of the virtues of a contented connubial relationship, while the determined, tight-lipped feminists mock this useless domesticity. Anna finally strikes out for India, where she will practice medicine among the poverty-stricken masses.

After several years there is another reunion. One marriage is wrecked by jealousy, another by boredom; but everyone involved rejects the thought of divorce. Anna has returned from India and informs her friends that she, too, has married. Finally, the shaky marriages somehow become marginally stabilized, and all the former members of the "Mädchenklub" fall into a pattern of tranquil contentment, their youthful zeal buried beneath an avalanche of "Kinder, Kirche und Küche."

Wedekind detested the accepted institution of marriage as much as he did the efforts of women to lose their femininity by avoiding sex altogether. In his animal hierarchy, the contented married woman was a "Schosshündchen" (lapdog), a domesticated animal who preferred, above all else, to sit at her husband's feet and dutifully obey the orders which Marguerite's Victorian spouse sternly gave her: "Never think about anything." These women are reduced to a pre-Nora state, and Wedekind makes several allusions to Ibsen's famous heroine, so as to underline his point. In one scene he obviously parodies Nora's addiction to macaroons. Ricarda is being hounded by a suitor but is desperately avoiding a commitment to marriage, knowing that her creative instincts will be stultified. The ardent young man urges her to accept a box of candy as a token of his love, but Ricarda, fully aware of the implications should she accept, time and again rejects the offer. But the mock chase ends with the capture of the prey, and the exhausted girl finally accepts the candy. With full awareness of the "symbolic" significance of her act, she ritually opens the box, slowly eats a delicate morsel and slumps down, another housewife.

Wedekind had no patience with women's emancipation clubs and what he considered their misdirected zeal. As one of the young men who constantly surround the girls point out, "Don't think that you can quench the thirst for activity with women's groups." For Wedekind, this was no more than a denial of their natural instincts. He felt that by honoring chastity, denying sexual life, and giving themselves a spurious choice of freedom or enslavement, they miss the essential truth and function of the female's existence. At the end, a tragic note is struck in this often silly dark comedy in that the girls sense their defection from what could have been a genuine emancipation movement: "We all deserve to be eaten by wild animals," says one, as she observes herself and her friends sinking into a life of dull mediocrity.

Ironically, Wedekind's most conscious anti-Naturalistic work remains his most naturalistic in structure and form. There is much of the situation comedy, a great deal of Shavian argumentation in a drawing room setting. But Wedekind's hand in characterization is somewhat stronger than Shaw's, and he is quicker to make what Wolfgang Kayser calls "the arbitrary distortion" of character. Wedekind reduces what in Shaw would have been parody to the level of puppetry, consciously manipulating his people to fit his needs, clearly acting out their parts under the explicit direction of the author. The stage is barren of flesh and blood, as Wedekind quite un-selfconsciously manipulates his lifeless cast of characters. In subsequent plays, this deliberate lack of characterization supports the fundamentally non-psychological nature of the action, but in *Die junge Welt* Wedekind's "children and fools" never attain a dimension which makes his unique style palatable. Here the inconsistencies of dialogue, thought, and action, all curiously out of touch with the normal world, seem pretentiously illogical.

Yet, for the student of Wedekind the play is obviously a portent of things to come. The dramatist has taken his language one step further. His characters are emerging as two-dimensional figures whose main function is to represent Wedekind's own point of view. The stage is serving as a sounding board for the expression of the artist's particular outlook, regardless of the necessities or niceties of dramatic convention. Wedekind is stepping further and further forward on the stage, establishing closer contact with his audience, explicitly stating what is on his mind, and instructing us accordingly. The development which led to the Epic Theater was most definitely underway.

Just one more word about the poet Meier. The group's dislike for him has given way to pity, for his poetry has driven him to a nervous breakdown. At the end, he remains one of the few unmarried young people, cursed, alas, by his ever-present notebook. Alma explains the difficulties involved in being courted by such a committed zealot: "When he kissed me, he always had his notebook with him, and with his free hand he would write down what I looked like at that moment. I got jealous of the notebook. . . When I asked, 'How did you sleep,' he would write it in his notebook. If I were to tell him he had driven over a child, he would write it in his notebook. When I pleaded with him to give up this goddam writing in his notebook, he would write it in his notebook." (II, 88)

## CHAPTER 4

# The Tragedy of Youth

AFTER having written three comedies of uneven accomplishment, with a suddenness which was totally unexpected Wedekind dramatically collected all of his creative forces and produced what is generally considered his most poetic and artistically most satisfying work, *Frühlings Erwachen*, completed in 1891. Once again he drew on his personal experience, betraying a tendency toward autobiographical drama which was to become a striking aspect of his later plays. From Wedekind's notebooks it is evident that his schooldays in Switzerland had made a profound impression on him, particularly the rash of suicides which inevitably took place toward the end of the academic year, when promotions were being decided. Wedekind's sympathy with the plight of the suffering adolescent fighting a stupid, tyrannical adult world stems from that period; and it was only a question of time before this profoundly moving theme found dramatic expression in his writings.[1]

Wedekind's orientation with regard to the torment of the teenager was, understandably, sexual. In this "Kindertragödie," he focuses on the sexual awareness which develops in youth, similar to his consideration of the problem in *Elins Erweckung*. But Wedekind adds another dimension to the conflict by underscoring the role of society in keeping its young people ignorant of their instincts. He launches a withering attack on the stupidity of the adult world, which righteously goes about the business of crushing everything which Wedekind considered beautiful and noble in youth.

The high school student Melchior Gabor is intellectually more advanced than his fourteen-year-old classmates, and the awakening of latent sexuality instinctively tells him that there is more to life than he has assumed. He is also fortunate in that his mother, an unusually liberal and understanding parent, has not engendered any feelings of guilt and shame; and Melchior is able to acquire a type of sexual education to prepare him for puberty. Partly through reading, but mostly through the observation of animals, he has gained a practical knowledge of sex and is convinced that if man were left untainted by civilization, he would follow the same primitive instincts which dominate the animal world on the lower orders. Love, marriage, and the other "conventions," he concludes, are not really a part of the elemental laws of nature.

Melchior's friends have not been as fortunate. Wendla Bergmann is told by her mother that the stork is responsible for making her an aunt. This explanation is given in the opening scene of the play, which sets the keynote for the children-adult conflict. The first words spoken symbolize the adult's effort to stifle and to "cover up" the physical beauties of the body.

Wendla: Why have you made my dress so long, mother?
Mrs. Bergmann: You're fourteen years old today.
Wendla: If I'd known you were going to make my dress as long as this,
    I'd rather not be fourteen. (II, 97)

Moritz Stiefel, Melchior's closest friend, is frightened and ashamed of the new feelings within him. He confesses to Melchior: "The last three weeks have been my Gethsemane." Moritz' sexual anguish is compounded by his fears of not being promoted. His entire life, as that of his classmates, depends on his advancement to the next class, Melchior aids his friend with his school work and also makes an effort to organize Moritz' understanding of his pubertal urges. He gives him a pamphlet he has written and illustrated, entitled "Co-habitation," explaining that "the entire world revolves around sex." But Melchior is himself not conditioned to deal with the matters he has discovered. He broods over his education, what he has heard from the adult world about such "immoral" feelings as are rising in him, and his passions explode. In Act II, scene four, he finds himself in a hayloft with the innocent Wendla, who has been instructed by her mother that people cannot have babies unless they are first in love with one another. He makes love to Wendla, who is driven on by emotions for which she has been totally unprepared.

Moritz has been promoted provisionally, but has failed to gain a permanent seat in the next class. Afraid of giving his parents the dreadful news, and frustrated in his efforts to flee to America, he finally turns to suicide. He contemplates this final act in a lonely woods; but his thoughts are interrupted by Ilse, a former schoolmate, who has broken from the vapid atmosphere of her home and is currently leading a wild, uninhibited existence in the midst of a large number of male admirers. Ilse is a sensual, animalistic, and thoroughly innocent creature, still another "fille de joie," in the service of animals of a lower order who do not necessarily appreciate her inner beauty but who lust after her nonetheless:

I've been faithful to the gang. Fehrendorf is an ape, Nohl is a pig, Bojowitch an owl, Loison a hyena, Oikonomopoulos a camel, yet I love them one and all and wouldn't want to be with anyone else even if the world were filled with angels and millionaires. (II, 140)

Ilse sincerely tries to save Moritz and urges him to join her band:

Moritz: I must go back, Ilse.
Ilse: Come as far as our house!
Moritz: What for?—What for?—
Ilse: We'll drink warm goat's milk! I'll curl your hair for you and hang a little bell around your neck. And there's a pony you can play with. (II, 140)

After a moment's temptation, Moritz rejects Ilse's offer, and she leaves him to his self-destruction. Among Moritz' belongings his parents find the manuscript given to him by Melchior. The school authorities are outraged and blame Mortiz' "perverse" act, which has brought shame on the school and on the parents of the deceased, on his friend's clinical account of copulation. In the most unforgettable scene in the play, Melchior is called before the executive committee of the school for judgment. Never again would Wedekind's grimly grotesque satire be as effective as here where he presents a group of idiotic, sadistic, and outrageously pedantic creatures attempting to mete out justice. They become involved in a debate concerning the merits of opening and closing the window, while Melchior waits patiently for the verdict. He is found guilty; and with the discovery that Wendla is pregnant, even his enlightened mother joins the collective outrage against him. His parents decide on a suitable punishment to spare society from the presence of this "animal": incarceration in a "Korrektionsanstalt." Wendla dies from an abortion forced on her by her mother. In the final scene, Melchior is shown as having escaped from the institution and wandering into a cemetery. He is haunted by thoughts of Wendla's death. Suddenly, from behind a tombstone steps Moritz, "with his head under his arm," to urge his friend that only in death could genuine peace be found:

> Moritz: We can do everything. Give me your hand! . . . It is peace, contentment, Melchior. You only need to stretch out one finger.
> Melchior: If I agree, Moritz, it will only be out of self-contempt. I see myself hated and detested by the world. All that gives me courage lies in the grave. . . To myself I am the most despicable person in the world. (II, 169–70)

Melchior is about to accept his friend's cordial invitation, when from behind still another tombstone steps "der vermummte Herr," who reveals to the death-desiring young man that his headless friend is a fraud who is miserable in death. This muffled gentleman now suggests that Melchoir come with him, not into the grave, but into the world of life and vitality: "I'll take you among men. I shall give you the opportunity to expand your horizon in the most fabulous way. I will acquaint you, without exception, with everything of interest which the world offers." (II, 171) Melchior asks the stranger to reveal his identity, thinking at first that it might be the devil, especially since much that he suggests has a particularly Mephistophelean quality. But he soon realizes that, unlike Moritz, He is "ein Mensch" and represents the affirmation of the life from which he was running. The gentleman takes Melchior's arm and leads him from his friend, out of the cemetery and back into life.

With this one play, Wedekind had begun a revolution in the modern theater, although few critics were aware of this fact at the time; and judging by the subtitle "eine Kindertragödie" it is conceivable that Wedekind himself did not fully understand the implications of his play. For to consider it as a "straight" tragedy is to place the work in jeopardy of ridicule. Klaus Völker agrees that as tragedy in the accepted tradition "the text would be awkward and ridiculous. The chief purpose of any production of the play can only be to underline the fantastic, bizarre humor."[2] Wedekind's tragic vision offered the stage a posture which it had not seen since Büchner, and the effect in the 1890's was no less incomprehensible than it had been seventy years earlier.

## I  *Enter the Absurd*

Wedekind's commitment to the cause of the children is so total that as realistic theater *Frühlings Erwachen* loses all perspective.

He was in no way interested in depicting a world normally motivated by the tragic events of a youth-adult conflict. The characterizations are strictly partial and un-selfconsciously partisan; there are no flawed individuals who might have evoked a sense of pity, even in their villainy. The enemy is the adult world, populated by brutes; and Wedekind's inspired repugnance explodes throughout the play. The schoolteachers above all reflect the mentality of this world, and their names produce a cacophony of ugliness: Sonnenstich (Sunstroke), Affenschmalz (Calflove), Knüppeldick (Cudgelthick), Hungergurt (Starveling), Knochenbruch (Bonebreaker), Fliegentod (Flykiller). Wedekind's treatment of other members of the adult Establishment is also reflected in their names: the school Porter Habebald (Catchemquick), the unctuously narrow-minded Pastor Kahlbauch (Skinnybelly), and the pompous and inane physician Dr. von Brausepulver (Seidlitz powder).[3]

Wedekind's two most venomous scenes dramatically underline the antithesis he wanted to demonstrate, the beautiful, lyrical sensitivity of the children in contrast to the wholly grotesque stupidity of their parents. Wedekind's ultimate weapon is distortion, and he carries his attack to the point where he abandons any semblance of rational behavior. The objects of his ridicule are absurd in both the traditional and modern meaning of the word. Wedekind most eloquently argues against the human condition simply by presenting his image of it, and his human aberrations, for all their madness, take on meaning. In Melchior's interrogation before a committee of his teachers investigating Moritz' death, and in the scene in which Moritz is buried, Wedekind approaches the level of fantasy and insanity found in the Dadaist theater twenty-five years later. Distortion, above all, was the key, and Wedekind found language to be his ultimate touchstone. He filled the mouths of his adults with the most colossal inanities which, in themselves, argued against identifying these puppets as human beings. In the first scene of Act III, the committee of teachers has gathered in the staff room, which has pictures of Pestalozzi and Rousseau hanging on the walls. Although they have ostensibly come together to examine Melchior's role in the death of his friend, they have already made up their minds:

Sonnenstich: Have any of the gentlemen any further remarks to make? Gentlemen, if we have no alternative but to apply to the Ministry of Education for the expulsion of our delinquent pupil, it is for the most weighty reasons that we do so. We do so because we must atone for the evil which has already befallen us and equally so because we must protect our institutions against similar calamities in the future. We do so because we must chastise our delinquent pupil for the demoralizing influence he has exercised upon his classmate; and above all we do so because we must prevent him from exercising this same influence upon the rest of his classmates. We do so—and this, gentlemen, may well be the weightiest reason of all—because we have the duty to protect our institution from the ravages of a suicide epidemic such as has already broken out in various other high schools, and which has till now set at nought all efforts to instil into the boys an awareness of the obligations of an educated existence by training them to be educated persons.—Have any of the gentlemen any further remarks to make?

Knüppeldick: Although fully in accord with Principal Sonnenstich's proposals, I can no longer resist the conclusion that the time has at last come to open a window somewhere.

Zungenschlag: I associate myself with the suggestion of my colleague Knüppeldick. The a-a-atmosphere which p-prevails here resembles that of an underground ca-ca-ca-catacomb, or the archives of the lawcourts in old Wetzlar.

Sonnenstich: Habebald!

Habebald: At your service, Sir!

Sonnenstich: Open a window! There is atmosphere enough outside, Thank God.—Have any of the gentlemen any further remarks to make?

Fliegentod: If my colleagues Zungenschlag and Knüppeldick wish to have a window opened all I ask is that it should not be the window immediately behind my back.

Sonnenstich: Habebald!

Habebald: At your service, Sir!

Sonnenstich: Open the other window! Have any of the gentlemen any further remarks to make?

Hungergurt: Without wishing to contradict our Principal, I would like to remind him of the fact that the other window has been bricked up since the autumn holidays. (II, 143–46)

Such is the level of discussion, while Melchior waits for the decision which will determine his future. But the clowning ceases when Melchior appears before them, and the futility of dealing with such grotesquely improbable types becomes nightmarish. He is confronted with the incriminating paper which Moritz had read and which is blamed for "the criminal's predisposing moral derangement." Whenever Melchior attempts to defend himself, he is brutally interrupted by the panel. The accused finds himself in a Kafkaesque courtroom, without defense or the means to argue his case. Melchior is rendered mute by the righteous onslaught of his teachers. What had been hilarious as these pedants argued among themselves over the virtues of opened windows as opposed to closed, now becomes surrealistically terrifying. Melchior's efforts at reason are futile in the face of society's irrational attack. Finally, he musters all of his strength for one supreme effort:

Melchior: I have written no more and no less than what are facts well known to you.
Sonnenstich: The scoundrel!
Melchior: I beg you to show me one offense against decency in the whole document!
Sonnenstich: Do you imagine I'm going to allow myself to be made a fool of by you in this way? Habebald. . . !
Melchior: I. . .
Sonnenstich: You have as little respect for the dignity of your assembled teachers as you have sense of decency towards man's instinctive feeling for modesty and discretion and a moral order of things!
Melchior: I. . .
Sonnenstich: I call upon our secretary, colleague Fliegentod, to close the minutes!
Melchior: I. . .
Sonnenstich: You are to be silent! Habebald!
Habebald: At your service, Sir!
Sonnenstich: Take him downstairs! (II, 147–48)

Justice is, of course, not available in Wedekind's world controlled by the Sonnenstichs. But the verbal nonsense which Wedekind insists that they indulge in loads the deck morally in favor of Melchior, whose efforts at moral honesty contrast with the narrowminded pedantry of his superiors. The scene takes on the quality of a medieval morality play, with characters representing definite precepts uncomplicated by subtleties of personality or action. Wedekind distills the qualities he wants, and, mixed with a strong emotional bias, presents them for the purpose of exposing themselves on the stage. Sonnenstich's sententious verbiage, his brutality in refusing to allow Melchior to speak, his outrage and moral indignation at Melchior's lack of "modesty and discretion" stretch the audience's credulity to the point where it becomes impossible to conceive of such a characterization in rational terms.

Wedekind draws the rest of the community into his net in the very next scene, in which Moritz Stiefel is buried. Here the grotesqueness is compounded by the nature of the funereal gathering, as the assembled mourners in turn vilify the suicide for his cowardly and shameful act:

Pastor Kahlbauch: He who denies the grace with which the Eternal Father has blessed those born in sin shall die the death of the spirit. —He who has lived and worked for evil in self-willed fleshy denial of the honor which is God's due, shall die the death of the body!— But he who lightly casts from him the cross which the All-merciful has laid upon him for his sins, verily, verily I say unto you, he shall die eternal death! — (*He throws a shovelful of earth into the grave.*) Let us who plod on and on the path of thorns praise the Lord, the All-bountiful, and thank him for the inscrutable disposition of His grace. For as surely as this man died a threefold death, as surely will our Lord God lead the righteous to bliss and everlasting life.— Amen.

Rentier Stiefel: The boy was no son of mine!—The boy was no son of mine! I never liked him, even as a child!

Sonnenstich (*throws a shovelful of earth into the grave*): Suicide, as the greatest conceivable transgression against the moral order of the universe, is the greatest conceivable proof of the existence of a moral order, in that the suicide saves the moral order the necessity of passing judgment and at the same time confirms its existence.

Knochenbruch (*throws a shovelful of earth into the grave*).

Uncle Probst (*throws a shovelful of earth into the grave*): I should not have believed my own mother if she had told me that a child could treat his parents so basely!

Friend Ziegenmelker (*throws a shovelful of earth into the grave*):—Could treat a father thus who for more than twenty years, early and late, had entertained no other thought than for the welfare of his child!

Pastor Kahlbauch (*pressing Rentier Stiefel's hand*): We know that to those who love God all things work together for good. I Corinthians, 12, 15.

Sonnenstich (*pressing Rentier Stiefel's hand*): We wouldn't have been able to promote him in any case.

Friend Ziegenmelker (*pressing Rentier Stiefel's hand*): Entrust yourself to my guidance:—What wretched weather, enough to make one's bowels quake! This sort of thing can affect the heart if one doesn't get hold of a hot grog pretty soon!

Rentier Stiefel (*blowing his nose*): The boy was no son of mine. . . The boy was no son of mine. (II, 149–50)

Wolfgang Kayser's comment is particularly incisive in regard to the author's treatment of the elders: "The caricatural distortion soon rises above the level of satire, makes itself independent, and transforms human beings into rigid, mechanically operated puppets. This arbitrary distortion, no longer prompted by the satiric impulse, determines the outward appearance of the characters, as well as their movements, thoughts, and language."[4] With dramatic contrast, Wedekind makes this world of distortion come into still sharper focus by introducing the children immediately after the adults have left the funeral, to pay their last respects to their deceased school friend. With all the bias and theatricality at his disposal, Wedekind permits his young people to perform without the burden of self-righteous pronouncement and smug resolution which systematically destroys any sense of identification with the older generation. The language of young people, in Wedekind's conception, must be at times lyrical, always honest, and painfully aware of the wretchedness of their existence:

Exit Rentier Stiefel, accompanied by Pastor Kahlbauch, Principal Sonnenstich, Professor Knochenbruch, Uncle Probst and friend Ziegenmelker. The rain abates.

Hänschen Rilow (*throws a shovelful of earth into the grave*): Rest in peace, you honest guy!—Give my best to my everlasting brides of sacrificial memory and commend me most devotedly to God in all His grace—you poor dope. They'll probably put a scarecrow on your grave in memory of your angelic simplicity. . .

Georg: Has the pistol been found?

Robert: No need to look for any pistol!

Ernst: Did you see him, Robert?

Robert: It's a damned fraud!—Who saw him?—Who?

Otto: That's just it. They'd covered him with a sheet.

Georg: Was his tongue hanging out?

Robert: His eyes!—That's why they'd covered him with a sheet.

Otto: Horrible!

Hänschen Rilow: It's your fault he's where he is. You called him a show-off.

Otto: Bull! I have to grind all night, too. If he had done his Greek literature, he wouldn't have needed to hang himself.

Ernest: Done your essay, Otto?

Otto: Only the introduction.

Ernst: I can't think of what to say.

Georg: Weren't you there when Affenschmalz assigned it?

Hänschen Rilow: I'll get something out of Democritus.

Ernst: I'll try to find something in Meyer's *Lexicon*.

Otto: Have you done the Virgil for tomorrow? (II, 151–52)

The boys leave, having no more time to worry or contemplate. The frightening realities of their school life push in on the temporary and

brief moment of thought about their comrade. They leave only Ilse
and another young girl, Martha, to play out the final tragicomic
moments in another outpouring of lyricism, humor, and grim horror:

(*The schoolboys leave.—Martha and Ilse approach the grave.*)
Ilse: Quick, quick! The gravediggers are coming.
Martha: Wouldn't it be better if we waited, Ilse?
Ilse: What for?—We can bring fresh ones. Fresh ones and then more
    fresh ones.—There are plenty more where these came from.
Martha: You're right, Ilse!—
(*She throws a wreath of ivy into the grave. Ilse opens her apron and lets
fall a great many fresh anemones onto the coffin.*)
Martha: I shall dig up our roses. I'll get beaten in any case.—Here they'll
    really grow!
Ilse: I'll water them whenever I come by. I'll bring forget-me-nots from
    the brook and irises from home.
Martha: It will be magnificent! Magnificent!
Ilse: I was just across the bridge there when I heard the shot.
Martha: The poor thing!
Ilse: And I know why he did it too, Martha.
Martha: Did he say something?
Ilse: Parallelepipedon! But don't tell anyone.
Martha: Cross my heart!
Ilse: Here's the pistol.
Martha: So that's why no one could find it.
Ilse: I took it out of his hand when I came by the next morning.
Martha: Give it to me, Ilse!—Please give it to me!
Ilse: No. I'm going to keep it as a souvenir.
Martha: Ilse, is it true that he's lying in there without a head?
Ilse: He must have loaded it with water.—The mulleins were sprinkled
    all over with blood. His brains were hanging from the willow
    branches. (II, 152–53)

Throughout these two scenes, as well as in the supernatural finale,
it becomes more and more apparent that Wedekind is attempting to
inculcate in his audience a point of view in which he passionately
believes. His primary purpose in creating this grotesque holocaust
is educational, to present, as Kayser suggests, "a perverted moral
tract."[5] As in no other of his works Wedekind is so clearly the zealot,
deliberately distorting his vision of the human condition to present
the allegory of good and evil. When Eric Bentley states that Wedekind's world is totally devoid of any morality, one might suspect that
he is missing the essential point of *Frühlings Erwachen*.[6] In this
bitter, often cynical diatribe against inhumanity, Wedekind collides
with the accepted puritanical morality of his age and advocates a

new standard of education, for adult and adolescent alike. But the traditional criticism for *Frühlings Erwachen* from the first was based on the assumption that the play was pornographic and obscene, and that its author nihilistically smashed the existing social order without supplying a substitute. Many years after the play became part of the repertory, a production could still cause a riot as, Anita Block informs us, occurred on the occasion of the American premiere.[7] That a cynical nihilism was furthest from Wedekind's thoughts can be seen simply from the dedication: "Dedicated by the author to the Man in the Mask," the force which repulses the dead Moritz and urges Melchior to reaffirm his belief in life and the power of man to change his world.

Wedekind's reputation as a pornographer dates from the earliest critical accounts of *Frühlings Erwachen,* and the stage history of the play is one involving censorship and official intervention; yet there is not a word of hard-core pornography in it, and as Kutscher points out, "it is quite clear that [Wedekind] went out of his way to avoid prurience."[8]

Wedekind's role as a moralist or amoralist can and will be debated as regards this play, but *Frühlings Erwachen* won for him a place in the modern theater. Wedekind reached back into the earlier part of the century to establish a line of continuity beginning with Georg Büchner and Christian Dietrich Grabbe.[9] He rejects any interest in depicting life as it is, in favor of articulating the artist's personal vision, which has scarcely any relationship to the natural, existing order.

Like Büchner and Grabbe before him, Wedekind ignored the rules of dramatic convention to create his unique idiom. In this case, the two conventional schools which he rejected were Realism and Naturalism, both cut basically from the same cloth. What Wedekind had to say was closely related to the manner in which he said it, and for that he needed "The Wedekind style," which for the first time came to complete fruition in *Frühlings Erwachen.* Deeply tragic scenes mingle with moments of hilarious farce; endless speeches mouthed by dehumanized marionettes are followed by the staccato dialogue of children-poets. Psychological and dramatic motivation disappears, as scene after scene races by in a whirling of dynamic tension. The stage is estranged from reality, as Wedekind begins a dramatic revolt resumed by Alfred Jarry's *Ubu Roi* in Paris five years later. Wedekind's *Frühlings Erwachen* represents the first volley of the theater's revolt which today shows little sign of abating.

## CHAPTER 5

# *The Paris Works: Circus and Varieté*

TO the extent that he absorbed his personal life into his literary activities, Wedekind is a delight to the literary historian. At no other period was this absorption so obviously manifested as during his "Pariser Zeit." Directly under the influence of his two antic friends Rudinoff and Gretor, Wedekind indulged himself to an extraordinary degree in the "non-intellectual" theater life of Paris. The little theater revues, "Grand Guignol" horror shows, popular pantomimes and, above all, the brilliant circuses constituted for him the ideal of what theater should be: untainted by civilization, "free from narrow-mindedness, pedantry, and anything unnatural."[1]

### I  Fritz Schwigerling (Der Liebestrank)

Wedekind's flexibility deserves mention at this point. He completely abandoned the poetic seriousness of his theme in *Frühlings Erwachen* to write what is his most enduring comic work.[2] *Fritz Schwigerling*, later renamed *Der Liebestrank*, was admittedly inspired by his fascination with the circus, and Wedekind poured into this farce all the gaiety which he could muster. He immortalized his friend Rudinoff in the character of Schwigerling, who embodies all the attractive qualities of the strong-man, bareback rider, ringmaster, and above all, the educator which Wedekind saw as the ultimate function of this exuberant figure. The hero demonstrates a tremendous vitality and elasticity which places him far above the maddening crowd of little people who dash about him. He is the doer, the activist, "der Tatmensch."

The improbable action of this comic melodrama takes place in imperial Russia, on the estate of Prince Ivan Michaelowitch Rogoschin near St. Petersburg. Rogoschin is a delightfully vulgar villain, a development of the type which Wedekind introduced in *Elins Erweckung*. The debauched nobleman has been made legal guardian of his deceased brother-in-law's only child, the beautiful nine-teen-year-old Katharina. In a plot which was to occupy millions of theatergoers during the silent-movie era, the wicked prince lusts after the innocent ward, scorning his devoted and patient wife. Rogoschin hires Schwigerling to aid him in his conquest, thinking that this "model of physical perfection and elasticity" could smooth the way for the seduction of the defiant Katharina, who wants no part of her guardian.

Fritz is the ultimate man-of-the-world, a Bohemian by nature who has wandered from the Folies Bergères to the circus, then to all corners of the world, educating people to the beauties of physical perfection and spiritual harmony. He is in every way the antithesis of the brutal prince and soon realizes to his disgust that the feudal Russian is no more than a predatory animal who must be deceived at any cost. Rogoschin wants him to prepare a love potion to smooth his way, and under the pretext of being her new tutor, he is intro-duced to his "subject." In her he sees more than the object of Rogo-schin's affections. She is the perfect pupil for his personal course in physical esthetics, the principle which has been the cornerstone of his mission in life. Through the appreciation of one's own bodily perfection, the individual attains harmony within himself:

Tickle ambition! Awaken self-esteem! In the circus one finds new con-cepts of education. An animal must acknowledge his pride in order to overcome any conceivable obstacle with dignity, with assurance. I relax the limbs, so that the spirit pulses through, so that freedom and joy quiver in every vein, until the wonder of it explodes in bright sparks from both eyes. The animal must swell his muscles and feel his breast heave when-ever he confronts the world. (II, 192)

Fritz has an instinctive affinity with the animal kingdom and basic distrust of culture and civilization, which he considers brutal, cruel, and the enemy of beauty. He sees in Rogoschin's tactics to subdue Katharina the epitome of this brutality. Rogoschin uses force, and his symbol is the whip, while Schwigerling instructs, cajoles, and attempts to inculcate a sense of dignity in his prize pupil, Katharina.

Katharina herself is a strange creature, an "animal" who is the object of the two methods of education. She is the only connecting link with *Frühlings Erwachen* in that her problem is her inability to understand the awakening forces within her. Katharina, like Fritz, prefers the company of beautiful animals to that of men, but unlike Schwigerling she is a raw, untouched creature, primitive in her sensibility and the ability to intellectualize the strength within her: "Every beating of my heart is like a pistol shot. I've ridden my horse into the ground; it doesn't help. I've tinkled away at Beethoven sonatas; it doesn't help. I've tamed wolves; it doesn't help. Life harbors some strange secrets which one cannot conceive of." (II, 193–94) Her only companion is a vulture in which she trusts more than any human.

Fritz' problem is twofold: successfully to deceive the prince without endangering his life, and to educate Katharina while channeling her energies to some useful purpose. He counters Rogoschin's brutality with wit, agreeing to concoct a love potion which will make the prince irresistible while rendering Katharina helpless. The slapstick comes fast and furious, especially while Schwigerling prepares the brew and sends Rogoschin off for some fairytale ingredients: the heart of the prince's favorite dog and the liver of a predatory bird, supplied conveniently by Katharina's pet. To the potion he adds the requirements that the elixir must be drunk in one gulp, and that the drinker must under no circumstances think of bears during the ritual, which is of course to assure that the simple-minded Rogoschin will indeed think of bears.

Meanwhile, Schwigerling begins to recognize his former associates all around him. In the chamberlain Colestin he discovers an old friend from Paris, a former actor at the Théâtre Français. Rogoschin's wife, the Princess Lisaweta, turns out to be, of all things, Schwigerling's first wife. They prepare a grand conspiracy to hoax the prince. Rogoschin interrupts them to complain that he can think of nothing but bears, and Schwigerling decrees an antidote. The Prince must sit for twenty-four hours, drinking tea and perspiring behind closed shutters. With the time gained through this deception, Katharina runs away with Schwigerling, to continue her training with her majestic "Tierbändiger" in the circus. Colestin, along with the chambermaid, joins them, and the prince returns bewildered to discover his empty castle, abandoned with the exception of the ever faithful Lisaweta, who kisses him consolingly.

Fechter has called *Der Liebestrank* "a witty grotesque," and there is a great deal of pure madness on stage, as well as some of Wedekind's most improbable characterizations. The princess is by far the most unsettling figure, as she stalks the stage in scene after scene. Pictures from some of the earliest productions show her hilariously costumed in a variety of circus outfits, a fat woman, middle-aged, most often dressed in tights. For she, too, is a creature of the circus.

After Fritz discovers, to his astonishment, that she was his first bride
—he went on to marry seven more times—she narrates the events
which led up to her marriage to Rogoschin: After Schwigerling there
came an American:

Princess: He was an American. A life insurance agent!
Schwigerling: Ha, the Yankee insured his precious life through you!
Princess: He got me an engagement with Barnum. Oh, he made millions
    with me. He treated me like no slave owner ever treated his most
    miserable victim. Night after night he made me do the Paphlagonian
    spring-dive.
Schwigerling (*sarcastically*): That's why he was a life insurance agent!
Princess: After I had broken all my ribs on Barnum's trapezes, he trained
    me to be a belly-dancer.
Schwigerling (*to himself*): The swine!
Princess: And so once again I became a star of the first magnitude on
    every stage in the Union. But he no doubt noticed that my beauty
    was fading. The monster came up with the plan to have me tatooed
    from top to bottom with hieroglyphics, in order to exhibit me at the
    Philadelphia Exposition as an Indian hostage; it was there that Rogo-
    schin appeared. My American spotted the prince immediately; be-
    sides, he was finished with me. He sold me off to Prince Rogoschin
    as "The Virgin from the Colorado River" for the fantastic sum of one
    hundred fifty-thousand dollars. (II, 228–29)

She dotes on Rogoschin, proclaiming to the world that he is just a
misunderstood little boy who is currently just going through a phase
—one which, alas, has lasted for most of his adult life. But she is
triumphant at the end, as she cradles her husband's head and whis-
pers: "You've still got me, the Virgin from the Colorado River!" (II,
249)

Schwigerling is the first fully developed "Kraftsmensch" created
by Wedekind, the author's conscious emissary on stage and the embodiment of the "Übermensch" as Wedekind saw him. He always is
the ringmaster, and with a magnificent flair, even in the grimmest
situations, is quite in control of matters. Schwigerling's interest in the
whole business is a passing one, an entr'acte, a sort of one-night
stand between his endless engagements. He is not governed by the
petty laws which rule other men, and as a result he is capable of
performing some incredible feats, as in the previous winter in Rome,
when he trained a Bengal tiger to play the hand-organ! He is also a
serious educational theoretician, and his esthetic principles are constantly serving as the foil to Rogoschin's alcoholic ravings.

Katharina is still another important forerunner of Lulu. Like Ilse she surrounds herself with the animal kingdom, but much more literally. She only has confidence in her animal friends, until Schwigerling comes along to advance her education. Before his arrival, she shared her food and lodging with her non-human friends only, but one by one the animals were driven off or killed by others. She is left alone, herself hunted: "The animals, thank God, are dead, except for one. But now the hunters are all going crazy running after her, just as they used to with their beasts." (II, 195) Schwigerling's main purpose is to make Katharina aware of the nobility of the animal feelings within her, to encourage pride in the instincts which she feels, and which distinguish her from the rest of mankind: "What we demand from *people* on the wire, trapeze, horizontal bar, or in the Roman circuses, that is what we attempt to awaken in the *animal* by means of the most careful, comprehensive education. The spirit, the soul, which slumbers in this beautiful organism, must come alive in a complete, harmonious expression." (II, 219)

In spite of the burlesque nature of the play, *Der Liebestrank* represents a significant aspect of Wedekind's art. There is a clear moral intent, an extension of the "Fleischmoral" of *Frühlings Erwachen* with its plea for sexual enlightenment. In *Der Liebestrank* Wedekind offers a companion esthetic to that of freedom from sexual oppression, as he argues for full appreciation of "the body's soul," as well as for the acceptance of physical spirituality as fundamentally more honest than the traditional sort. As in his earlier plays, the implication is obvious: civilization denies man his instincts.

## II  *Pantomimes and Ballets*

It was merely a short step from the esthetics of motion of *Der Liebestrank* to a more complete expression of physical perfection and grace. Wedekind's interest in the ballet was a natural outcome of his Parisian experience, as well as the revived interest in this art form which Nietzsche initiated. It was in Nietzsche most likely that Wedekind found the spiritual connection between his own innate theories of physical beauty and the rejection of civilization as a positive force.[3] His four pantomimes represent the absolute abandonment of the limitations imposed by theatrical necessity in favor of a Dyonisian primitivism of pure theater. Wedekind leaped over two thousand years back to the original nature of the dance as a religious experience of erotic conception and fantasy. These works are totally physical as well as imaginative. It appears that Wedekind, in his contempt for the language of civilization, adopted a form which freed him from the necessities of any sort of intellectual articulation. Gesture and the physical motion of the dance were his only tools here, and the intent was to employ these to revive the mythic, sensual nature of the ancient dance form as it was recognized in pagan times. It should come as no surprise that, of all of Wedekind's works, his pantomimes are by far the most erotic and overtly sexual.

*Die Flöhe, oder Der Schmerzentanz* (*The Fleas, or the Dance of Pain*), was originally written in French, later translated by Wedekind and included in the collection of prose and poetry, entitled *Fürstin Russalka,* which appeared in 1897.[4] Maria Leczinska, Queen of France, is riding with her six-year-old daughter through the Boulogne Forest on the road to Versailles. The entourage is interrupted by an old crone who hypnotizes everyone and carries off the child. For two years the distraught queen searches in vain for her daughter, and the courtiers, concerned for her health, devise an entertainment to buoy up her spirits. They hire Professor Paolo Pandulfo Pantaleone from Padua (known from *Der Schnellmaler*) and his flea circus. During the performance at court, one of the fleas, a soloist, signals the other performers, and they suddenly dash beneath the skirts of the court ladies as well as the queen. In an uproariously funny music hall scene the bitten ladies tear off their dresses and dance a wild cancan in their undergarments. The tormented ladies retreat to their bedrooms, where they are consoled by the courtiers. When the tormenting fleas slip from beneath the beds for a conference, they are captured and imprisoned, with the exception of the soloist, who is discovered sleeping contentedly under the queen's covers. She refuses to part with the ugly creature, kisses it, and sees it transformed into her daughter. Professor Pantaleone receives compensation for his lost flea, and everyone, as is only fitting in such a fairytale atmosphere, lives happily ever after.

In his ballets as nowhere else Wedekind approached the doctrine of "Art for Art's Sake"; and, certainly, *Die Flöhe* is a break in Wedekind's moralizing posture. It is light and frivolous, and yet one detects certain hallmarks of the Wedekind stagecraft. The bizarre academician–animal-trainer Pantaleone is a composite mutant of Schwigerling and the teachers from *Frühlings Erwachen.* Since he was unable *to speak* of animals, Wedekind simply filled the stage with them, and the chorus of fleas gives the work the flavor of a romantic bestiary, much like the menageries encountered in the preceding plays. But, above all, there is the emphasis on motion.

Wedekind's directions for the technical aspects of the ballet are surprisingly professional and specific, and the pantomime is constantly punctuated by a wide variety of classical ballet dances, as well as those more often found in the music halls of Paris.

In *Der Mückenprinz* (*The Mosquito Prince*), Wedekind combines the romantic fairytale with the highly ritualized flavor of a pagan sexual rite. The ballet, which appeared in the *Fürstin Russalka* collection and later in the novel *Mine-Haha,* opens with a pastoral scene in which farm girls are dancing with a swarm of mosquitos in a welcome to spring.[5] Prince Leonor enters the wood with a net and captures the leading male mosquito, after killing a female. With the mosquito caged, Leonor cavorts with Lina, one of the farm girls. The magician Hächi-Bümbüm approaches with his daughter, and Leonor brutally throws off Lina in favor of his new enamorata, to whom he presents the caged mosquito as a token of his love. With the blessings of the father, Leonor announces his engagement to the magician's daughter, Ada. The wedding procession takes place in a room where a huge golden bed has been prepared for the newlyweds. After the feast, the courtiers leave, and Ada embraces her husband, who unexpectedly finds himself soon bored and exchanges her with the mosquito in the cage.

Leonor then escorts one of the court ladies to his bed, but she is stung by the mosquito, and her stomach begins to swell. Leonor now drives this unfortunate lady out and reappears with Lina as his new partner. This time, the mosquito turns on the prince, and when his own stomach begins to swell, he furiously locks the insect in the cage with his wife. In the final scene a doctor is called in to administer to the prince's swollen stomach. He performs a grotesque operation which does not relieve Leonor's discomfort and is summarily killed. Prince Leonor, in a rage, drags his wife from the cage and orders his servant to get into the bed with her. Taking out all his anger on poor Ada, he commands his courtiers to trample her. But the old magician finally intervenes and casts a spell over the entire company, which causes everyone to run around the room on his hands. This German Prospero now transforms the mosquito into a man, and after the mosquito swarm has stung Leonor to death, Ada mounts the bed with her newly created lover.

If anything, this strangely chaotic work indicates that Wedekind very definitely knew what suggestive eroticism was all about. Phallic symbols, swelling stomachs, the bed as central metaphor, all point to the conscious sexuality which Wedekind intended to convey. The most striking feature, however, is the lavish pageantry. Wedekind's detailed instructions for costume and scenery for the bedroom wedding procession remind one of an elaborate Elizabethan masque.

Yet the sexuality is not bereft of "message." There is the villainy of Prince Leanor to point to the evilness of sexual aberration as Wedekind saw it, the brutality and soullessness of the predatory sexual variant, a pervert in Wedekind's eyes, who approaches sex with ugliness and a total lack of understanding. His violence is punishable by death.

As always, there is comic relief, this time not destructively satirical as with the teachers in *Frühlings Erwachen* or ridiculous as with the old pedant in *Die junge Welt*. The magician with the improbable name and antic actions is portrayed as a type of academician—Wedekind's favorite target—but like his Shakespearean model in *The Tempest*, his white magic saves the day.

Although *Die Kaiserin von Neufundland* (*The Empress of Newfoundland*) rivals Wedekind's other ballets in the degree of unrestrained imagination, there is much more that one would describe as vintage Wedekind.[6] As is obvious from the title itself, Wedekind indulges in his peculiar interest in the New World, which, at least in this work, has very little to do with the nature of the plot or characterization; and with the unmotivated appearance of the inventor Thomas Alva Edison, the zany Americanism begins to look like eccentricity.

But more central is the main story, which deals with a woman's effort to fulfill her overwhelming sexual appetite (why this should happen to take place in Newfoundland is best answered by another question: why not?). Princess Filissa is pining away for the love of a man; no particular one, but her search takes on the characteristics of a desperate contest to find *the* man who might give her happiness. Doctors examine her and offer somber medical advice: "Marry or die!"[7] Various candidates appear to compete for the honor of marrying the sad princess. The poet Pustekohl, after reciting some ridiculous verse, is laughed out of the hall. The next two esteemed individuals also fail: Napoleon Bonaparte and Edison only bore her to sleep!

Just as she is about to give up the search for a mate, the princess is electrified by the great feats of strength of Holtoff, a weight-lifter, and selects him as the ideal specimen. She showers him with extravagant gifts, stripping her citizens of their wealth to supply him with favors. The poet, still hoping to impress the empress, commits suicide in front of her, but to no avail. When Holtoff lives two thousand kilograms, the empress' joy is so complete and violent that it becomes necessary to lock her up.

But Holtoff is no more than a brute with a beautiful body, another of Wedekind's soulless male animals, "Fleisch ohne Geist." He debases Filissa, finally abandoning her, and in the last scene he is found in a bar in the company of admiring vagabonds, sailors, and assorted prostitutes. The humiliated but unsatiated empress crawls in. To give her one final thrill, he condescendingly agrees to lift once more. But Holtoff's debauchery has destroyed him as well, and his body now fails him. For Filissa there is only one act which can satisfy her needs, and she begs Holtoff to kill her. He is too preoccupied with his own inability to lift the weight, and in a final demonic surge she strangles herself with her own hair.

Wedekind is back once again with the theme of his "Geist-Fleisch" morality. Physical beauty alone, as with the brainless Holtoff, is useless without the accompanying spiritual awareness of Schwigerling. Filissa is also not the ideal, for Wedekind treats her sexual excesses in a most absurd fashion. She seems a conscious parody, a caricature of the innocent and honest sensuality of the later Lulu as well as the earlier "Freudenmädchen," and Wedekind's grotesque treatment of "the lovers" is distinctly mocking in tone. In the final scene, as Filissa begs Holtoff to drop a huge weight on her, he genuinely tries to do so. He strains to get the fifty-pound trifle off the ground, but before he can drop it on his wife the weight falls on his foot, and the bumbling strongman goes hopping around the bar, holding his damaged leg. Immediately thereafter Filissa strangles herself.

*Die Kaiserin von Neufundland* is more varieté than ballet, with a generous amount of *Grand Guignol* cruelty thrown in. Wedekind places the emphasis on the comic side at the expense of his otherwise serious exposition of sexual themes, and the resulting cynicism, as Kutscher admits, is out of balance.

### III  *Once Again: America*

Wedekind's last ballet, "Die grosse Pantomime *Bethel*," is also his most complete statement of his image of America, and it is one which, strangely enough, proves to be the most lasting of these four astonishing dance pieces.[8] He presents a fantastically disfigured view of the New World and its inhabitants, with no attempt at gaining an understanding of national characteristics. *Bethel* is a series of grotesquely wild scenes depicting the life and times of a trotting

horse, who gives her name to the title. The schemings of her un-
scrupulous American owners take place at race tracks on both sides
of the Atlantic, in American bars, and finally conclude "in the vicin-
ity of Sioux-City, Nebraska" (sic). Among the strange events which
are acted out is the heavyweight championship boxing match between Bob Fitzsimmons and James Corbett, which actually did take
place at Carson City, Nevada, in 1897. Wedekind calls for a cast of
"Irische Barmaids, Niggers, Kavaliere, Chinesen, Siouxindianer,
Sportsmen, Buchmacher, Losverkäufer, Jockeys . . . American Girls,
Nigerinnen, Chinesinnen, Indianerinnen . . . drei Festwagen mit den
Figuren der New-Yorker Freiheitsstatute, Georges Washingtons,
Lafayettes, Lincolns, Booths, Uncle Sams, usw. usw." (IX, 71)
Throughout the general pandemonium, a constant stream of circus
animals, fat men, clowns, and horse-back riders perform often with
little concern for the actual plot. The work is incredibly crude and
often offensive, and portrays America as a moral swamp of materialism ruled by cunning capitalists and vulgarly stereotyped minority
groups. As expected, the caricature also extends to several excep-
tionally inept academic and medical types.

What was Wedekind's American vision? If anything, his "complex"
has an extraordinary number of facets. From the references in *Die
junge Welt,* Wedekind quite obviously considered the United States
to be much more liberal in matters of education than Europe; and
the several references already mentioned point to his desire to travel
to America. But the other side of the coin is complete distortion, an
image which, in the literature of the twentieth century, as instanced
by Brecht and Dürrenmatt, became the more accepted view.[9] In
*Bethel* Wedekind first articulated this grotesquely ugly image which
became the model for his disciples.

Wedekind's use of pantomime represents an important step for him
and for the development of the art form itself. Initially, it is the cul-
mination of his efforts to escape the drab, sociologically based theater
of his generation. By withdrawing completely from the necessities
of verbal expression he was able to minimize the importance of
language. As Fritz Strich puts it: "His urge for elemental nature
found here its un-literary form. The confidence in the body's power
of expression, which had been ignored for so long, the pleasure of
rhythm awakened in him and displaced the necessity for words."[10]
Wedekind's indifference to psychological motivation leads quite naturally to the destruction of the traditional use of language as the
sole means of communication.[11]

Where does this subordination of the spoken word lead to? From Wedekind's effort to establish a new set of criteria in order to affect the audience and to satisfy his own inner need for artistic creation, the line goes directly to Antonin Artaud's *The Theatre and Its Double*. Written in 1938, Artaud's manifesto became the revolutionary handbook for the dramatist of revolt.[12] Artaud wrote: "Here is what is really going to happen. It is simply a matter of substituting for the spoken word a different language of nature, whose expressive possibilities will be equal to verbal language, but whose source will be tapped at a point still deeper, more remote from thought."[13] Artaud discovered in the mime the anti-psychological force he felt was essential for the creation of a new vitality in the theater. To a most revealing extent, however, Wedekind anticipated Artaud's ideas and incorporated them actively into his own dramas. In dealing with Wedekind's Lulu plays, we shall seek to demonstrate that almost all of Artaud's principles and theories found their initial expression in the plays of Wedekind.

# CHAPTER 6

# *Lulu*

". . . We shall try to concentrate, around famous personages, atrocious crimes, super-human devotions, a drama which, without resorting to the defunct images of the old Myths, shows that it can extract the forces which struggle within them."

Antonin Artaud

UP to this point in his development, Wedekind had concentrated on male characters in employing either spokesmen or ideal types to represent his moral and philosophical position. Through Elin, Melchior, Moritz, the "vermummte Herr," Schwigerling on one hand, and a whole series of uncompromising villains depicting bourgeois society on the other, Wedekind's vision of the conflict between civilization and freedom appeared male-oriented. But there were also significant female counterparts to his defiant men. Schigolch's daughter in *Elins Erweckung,* Ilse in *Frühlings Erwachen,* Katharina, and even the Empress in *Die Kaiserin von Neufundland,* are variations of "das Freudenmädchen," women born for pleasure who can find means to express their need only outside the normal channels of society.

Wedekind now turned all of his attention to his image of the woman's role in society. As early as *Die junge Welt,* it was evident that, typically, he was running counter to the mainstream of the women's emancipation movement and the efforts of the female to "defeminize" herself. The only other contemporary writer to deal with the problem of the "Eternal Feminine" was August Strindberg, but ultimately Strindberg's combativeness in such matters led him to assume his legendary negative attitude. For him the power of the female over the male was a destructive force, violently undermining the survival of humanity. In his plays and novels, a similar status is given to the woman; she has been elevated to a role of mythic proportions. As in Wedekind's works, Strindberg's mythical treatment takes on the nature of a sexual struggle, with the resulting victory of the female's sexual drive destroying a helplessly struggling male victim. But Strindberg laments this situation, whereas Wedekind glorifies it. It is the instinctive power of Eros which, for Wedekind, could rid civilization of its repressiveness. As in *Die junge Welt*, he particularly deplores and ridicules those women who would attain equality with men by voluntarily denying their womanhood. Wedekind saw beyond the artificiality of what he considered to be the fraud of the feminine mystique of his day, "Frau" and "Weib," to a more elemental level: "Das schöne, wahre Tier," the beautiful and genuine animal in the female of the species. In an effort to embody this principle, Wedekind created his Lulu as the personification of the eternal struggle between sex and society.

## I Erdgeist

With the exception of Goethe's Gretchen, no female in all of German literature has received as much attention as Wedekind's Lulu, and thanks to Alban Berg's opera, she is currently once more enjoying a renaissance. Lulu has been labeled by countless critics: fleshly lust personified; the female, around whom whirls the grotesque dance of death; woman in her most primitive form; the soulless feminine animal; a mythic force incomprehensible to those who lust after her.[1] It is with Lulu that henceforth Wedekind's name would be inevitably linked, and it is because of her that from the time of her creation his name was invariably associated with the charge of obscenity.

Lulu was Wedekind's single most imposing symbol of his fight against civilization. She represents the antithesis of a civilized society, someone totally alien to the everyday world of reality. Lulu represents for Wedekind mankind in his precivilized state, innocent and unpsychological, instinctive and supercharged with a strength which has become sublimated in modern society. In its present form, society has progressed to the stage where the likes of Lulu have been purged. Civilization had bypassed the instincts, Wedekind felt. In creating her and by placing her once again into the mainstream of a civilization which had progressed beyond her, Wedekind was hoping to establish a conflict.

The result is a brutal collision of intelligence and primal instinct, with no holds barred. For a time, anarchy runs loose on the stage. In this struggle between the unknown and the known, psychological meaning, accepted realities, and discursive thought are condemned, as Wedekind weaves the fabric of his theater of cruelty.

Wedekind originally conceived of his Lulu play as one gigantic work, which he began writing in 1892. This "gigantic tragedy" was called *Die Büchse der Pandora* (*Pandora's Box*), and Wedekind sent it complete to Albert Langen in the summer of 1895. The play proved much too unwieldy, and eventually Wedekind broke it up into two plays, as we now have it: *Der Erdgeist* and *Die Büchse der Pandora*. His immediate inspiration came from two sources: the sensational crimes of Jack the Ripper, who had terrorized London several years earlier, and which Wedekind probably saw dramatized at the Grand Guignol; and from a pantomime by Felicie Champsau, *Lulu, une Clownesse Danseuse*, which he saw at the Nouveau Cirque in Paris.

The title of *Der Erdgeist* hints at the mythic nature of the subject matter which Wedekind intends to deal with, and he never lost sight of this *grandeur*. Wherever possible Wedekind reinforces the allegorical and symbolic sense of his theme, and nowhere is this more evident than in a Goethe-like Prologue—naturally not set in heaven, but in a Wedekindian circus sideshow: "The curtain rises to disclose the entrance to a tent from which emerges, to the sound of cymbals and the beating of drums, an animal tamer dressed in a vermilion red frock-coat, white tie; he has long black curly hair, white breeches and top-boots; in his left hand he carries a riding whip, in his right a loaded revolver."[2] The ringmaster-animal trainer, speaking directly to the audience, offers the viewers the opportunity to see life as it really is, not the false mirror, alas, which the majority of theatergoers prefer:

> The times are bad. Ladies and gentlemen
> Who once would crowd before my cage's show
> They honour farces, dramas, operas, Ibsen,
> With their most estimable presence now—(III, 8)

Gradually, the ringmaster is transformed into Wedekind himself, as he denounces Ibsen and Hauptmann, the latter in a thinly veiled reference to *Vor Sonnenaufgang*:

> What do these plays of joys and griefs reveal?
> Domestic beasts, well-bred in what they feel,
> Who vent their rage on vegetarian fare
> And then indulge in a complacent tear,
> Just like those others—down in the parterre.

> This hero cannot hold his liquor in,
> This one's uncertain if his love is genuine.
> You hear the third despair of this earth-ball
> (For five long acts he groans about it all),
> None gives the coup de grace to do him in. (III, 8)

Only in this menagerie can the audience be exposed to genuine life:

> The wild and lovely animal, the true,
> Ladies and gentlemen, only I can show you.

At this point Lulu is carried in by a strongman and introduced to the onlookers:

> She was created for every abuse,
> To allure and to poison and seduce,
> To murder without leaving any trace.
> Sweet creature, now keep in your proper place,
> Not foolish nor affected nor eccentric,
> Even when you fail to please the critic.
> You have no right with miaows and spits inhuman
> to distort for us the primal form of woman,
> With clowning and with pulling stupid faces
> To ape for us the childlike simple vices. (III, 9–10)

With a final flourish of pistol shots and caresses, the ringmaster has "our snake" carried back behind the curtains, and the play begins, as he "steps back into the tent to the sound of cymbals and the beating of drums."

The play itself opens with an ornately realistic setting, the studio of the artist Schwarz, who has been commissioned to paint the portrait of the fiancée of the powerful newspaper publisher Dr. Ludwig Schön. Their conversation turns to another picture on which Schwarz is working; a picture of Lulu, whose jealous husband, Dr. Goll, has had her pose as Pierrot in a provocative white ballet costume. Schön immediately recognizes "the sweet creature" and tells Schwarz of his first encounter with her. He had found her on the streets as a child, educated her and cared for her, and recently married her off to Goll, whom he knew would keep a strong rein on her. Finally Lulu appears and, when left alone with the painter, finds herself chased around the studio by the enamored Schwarz, until she collapses on the sofa. The somewhat hysterical painter is covering Lulu with kisses when Goll knocks at the door and, finding it locked, kicks it in and rushes at the compromised pair on the couch. He is about to strike Schwarz, but is seized with a heart attack and dies at their feet. Schwarz is hysterically helpless as he stands over Goll's corpse, desperately trying to get Lulu to understand the seriousness of their situation. But she finds little to excite herself about. After failing to relate her to the horror of Goll's death, Schwarz attempts to discover exactly *what* Lulu is:

> Schwarz: Look me in the eyes!
> Lulu: What are you after?
> Schwarz: Look me in the eyes!
> Lulu: I can see myself as a pierrot in them.
> Schwarz: This damned dancing!
> Lulu: I must go and change.
> Schwarz: There's one thing I want to ask you. . .
> Lulu: But I mustn't answer.
> Schwarz: Can you speak the truth?
> Lulu: I don't know.
> Schwarz: Do you believe in a creator?
> Lulu: I don't know.
> Schwarz: Is there anything you can swear by?
> Lulu: I don't know. Leave me alone. You're mad.
> Schwarz: What do you believe in, then?
> Lulu: I don't know.
> Schwarz: Have you no soul, then?
> Lulu: I don't know.
> Schwarz: Have you ever been in love?
> Lulu: I don't know.
> Schwarz: She doesn't know! (III, 33)

Lulu does not know because she cannot know. She is not a creature of this world. Lulu is flesh and blood, but her humanity and her ability to reason end there. Schwarz's probing is meaningless to her, because she is incapable of judgment and above all, of feeling, since she has no sense of sin or guilt. As Schön had mentioned, no one knew where she came from, she has no mother or father, and there is nothing and no one to whom she is related. At the end of the first act, Wedekind has established Lulu's role. To each man she is something else, and, indeed, each one has a different name for her: Nelli, Eva, Mignon, besides Lulu. This multiplicity is derived from the fantasy of each male who associates with her, and each man's fate is determined by his reaction to her. She herself is no more than the principle of the arch-female, "with a smile on her lips and nothing in her heart."³

Lulu has become Schwarz's wife in the second act. His joys are boundless, a result of his blissful happiness with Lulu and the sudden popularity of his paintings, which have been given an unwarranted amount of praise in Schön's publications. He loves Lulu with a naïvely sentimental passion: "Every day I feel as if I were seeing you for the first time." In the midst of Schwarz's marital paradise, a caller appears, a mysterious old man named Schigolch, who introduces himself as Lulu's father-protector, and to whom Lulu confides as she does to no other human being. When they are momentarily left alone, Lulu complains bitterly about her life with her husband:

> Schigolch: Does he drink?
> Lulu: Not yet.
> Schigolch: Does he hit out?
> Lulu: No, he goes to sleep.
> Schigolch: When he's drunk you can examine his entrails.
> Lulu: I'd rather not. (III, 39)

Lulu received more pleasure even from old, irascible Dr. Goll, who treated her like a caged animal. She cannot abide the bourgeois love of the painter; and to Schön she pours out her disgust for her husband—"He loves me!"— which for Lulu is the most contemptuous statement she is capable of making. Schön is now officially engaged and wishes to break all ties with Lulu, who has been visiting him regularly. In Schön, Lulu sees a man who could offer her the strength and vitality to match her own, but this man of action wants no more than respectability, free from the powerful passions of Lulu. Schön realizes that Schwarz will be unable to cope with Lulu unless he strengthens his hold on her, and that an unhappy Lulu will always be a threat to him. He goes directly to his task and confronts Schwarz with the truth of Lulu's background, further informing him that his fame is due solely to the publicity which Schön has given his paintings. His advice to the stunned artist is impossible, given the nature of Schwarz's love:

> Schön: Let her feel your authority. She asks nothing better than to render
> unconditional obedience. She was blissfully happy with Dr. Goll, and
> he wasn't a man to stand any nonsense.
> Schwarz (*shaking his head*): She said she'd never been in love.

Schön: But you must begin with yourself. Pull yourself together.

Schwarz: She swore to me.

Schön: You can't demand any sense of duty from her as long as you fail to recognize where your own task lies.

Schwarz: By her mother's grave!!

Schön: She didn't know her mother, let alone her grave. Her mother has no grave. (III, 52–53)

But with his ideals shattered, Schwarz is unable to cope with Lulu as he now sees her. Overwhelmed with self-pity and ludicrous in his own bathos, he calms himself for the moment, leaves the room, and cuts his throat. Schön, after his discovers the body, is momentarily gripped by the fear that Lulu has unalterably hooked him. His main concern, as he takes his turn in ruminating while standing over the corpse, is the scandal which might result from this suicide, and the effect on his engagement. He is shocked out of his stupor when his son Alwa races in with the news that revolution has broken out in Paris. Schön is once again in control, the man of action, as he calmly dictates to a reporter the story of Schwarz's end: "Take this down. . . Persecution mania. . ." Next to him stands Lulu, sprinkling her handkerchief with scent and wiping the blood from Schön's hand. (III, 59)

The confrontation between Lulu and Schön now becomes the main source of the tension, as she sets about gaining possession of the only individual capable of withstanding her power.

In order to find still another husband for Lulu, Schön hands her over to his son, who is producing one of his own ballets and uses Lulu in the leading role. While enjoying tremendous popular acclaim, Lulu is dancing only for Schön, who feels his strength draining away. He is still engaged, but his determination to resist Lulu is undermined by a growing hysteria on his part. On seeing him in a private box with his fiancée, Lulu faints on stage, and when Schön rages backstage to force her back to the performance, he finally capitulates. After resorting to insults, Schön is about to beat her into submission:

Schön (*raising his fist*): God forgive me. . .

Lulu: Strike me! Where is your whip? Strike me across the legs!

Schön (*his hands to his temples*): Away! I must get away! (*Rushes to the door, pulls himself together, turns back.*) Can I appear before the child like this?—I must go home.—If only I could escape from the world itself!

[ 70 ]

Lulu: Be a man.—Look yourself in the face for once.—You haven't a
scrap of conscience.—You do just as you please—and you know as
well as I do—that. . .
Schön (*has sunk down utterly exhausted into the chair*): Stop!
Lulu: That you're too weak—to free yourself from me. . . (III, 76–77)

Lulu breaks his will, destroys all of Schön's hopes of finding the
tranquillity of a normal life, and in a parody of Schiller's *Kabale und
Liebe,* Lulu dictates the letter to Schön which is to end his engagement—and his life:

Schön: For God's sake, tell me what I am to do.
Lulu (*gets up. Her cape remains on the chair. She pushes aside the cos-
tumes on the center table*): Here is writing paper. . .
Schön: I couldn't write. . .
Lulu (*standing behind him, her hand on the arm of his chair*): Write:
"My dear Countess". . .
Schön (*hesitating*): I call her Adelaide. . .
Lulu: "My dear Countess". . .
Schön: My death-sentence!
Lulu: "You must take back your word. I cannot reconcile it with my
conscience"—(*as Schön puts down the pen and looks at her implor-
ingly*) write "reconcile it with my *conscience,* to link you with my
unhappy existence.". . .
Schön: You're right.—You're right.
Lulu: "I give you my word that I am unworthy of your love." (*As Schön
again turns aside.*) Write "of your love. These lines will prove it to
you. I have been trying to break away for three years; I have not the
strength. I am writing to you at the side of the woman who dominates
me. You must forgive me."—
Schön (*groaning aloud*): Oh God!
Lulu (*half frightened*): Don't say that! (*with emphasis*) "Dr. Ludwig
Schön."—Postcript: "Do not attempt to rescue me."
Schön (*collapses as he finishes writing*): Now—for the—execution. . .
(III, 78)

Lulu has won, and the last act is more or less anticlimactic. As
Schön's wife, she displays the same boredom and indifference that
marked her life with her former husbands. The fun was in the challenge, and having conquered, Lulu looks elsewhere for excitement.
She finds it by turning Schön's home into a bizarre watering hole
for her strange clan of acquaintances. Besides Schigolch, there is
Rodrigo Quast, a pompously arrogant strongman (one of Wedekind's beautiful bodies bereft of spirit); young Hugenberg, a roman-

tic student at the Gymnasium; Countess Geschwitz, a lesbian devoted to Lulu; a variety of servants, as well as Schön's son Alwa.

They all have one thing in common: the desire to possess Lulu. Together they enjoy the grotesque game of Schön's humiliation. Whenever he appears, they hide behind whatever object is available. As soon as he turns his back, curtains, tables, and screens pour out a steady stream of suitors in the most outrageous slapstick fashion. His personal tragedy is made all the more bizarre, as he plays out his role as overseer to a Marx Brothers' madhouse. The man of elasticity is at his wits' end, and in a moment of desperation he hands Lulu a gun, hoping that she will kill herself and end his misery. But even his last effort to gain freedom ends in farce, but farce with a grotesque overtone. As Lulu—holding the pistol—and Schön confront each other, the frightened Hugenberg screams from beneath the table; and as Schön whirls to identify the source of this distraction, Lulu fires five shots at her husband "and continues to pull the trigger." As the police arrive, Alwa is holding Lulu in his arms, and Hugenberg utters the last improbable lines of the play: "I shall be expelled from school." (III, 97)

What is Wedekind attempting to show in *Erdgeist*, and what is the best way of approaching this astonishing work? Certainly, the central issue is Lulu and her relationship to society. Wedekind makes this point in the prologue, and he never really deviates from it. He presents two unalterable forces on a collision course. There is no hope at a compromise, because there exists no sense of understanding between these two forces. Goll and Schön consider her an animal, a bestial subhuman which must be controlled at all costs. Worse still, the pathetic artist Schwarz treats her simply as a beautiful woman, to be loved and admired. For a time, even Schigolch advises Lulu to accept the role of "das schöne Tier" as the best sort of accommodation to society, but she is instinctively unable to make any concessions at all. She can only function in the way she has been created, following her nature. To the individual who functions in a social context, this may seem no more than "demonic sexuality." But the sexual is always underplayed with Lulu. There is nothing "dirty" about her, and in the sequel, *Die Büchse der Pandora,* when she must resort to prostitution to support her cronies, the act seems thoroughly incongruous.

Lulu does not belong to the "normal" world and should not be judged by the values it cherishes. Her mysterious background, the strange relationship with Schigolch—the only man over whom she has no influence—which borders on the supernatural, and the very title of the play would seem to make Wedekind's allegorical intent obvious. Schigolch understands her completely, and Lulu senses his presence even before he physically arrives on the scene, as in Act II, scene one:

(*A bell rings outside in the passage*)
Schwarz (*with a start*): Damn!
Lulu: Nobody at home!
Schwarz: Perhaps it's the picture dealer.
Lulu: It can be the Emperor of China for all I care.
Schwarz: Just a minute. (*Exit.*)
Lulu (*as one seeing a vision*): You?— You?— (*Closes her eyes.*)
Schwarz (*coming back*): A beggar, who says he was in the wars. (III, 38)

Wedekind completes the alienation of Lulu from society by distorting the "civilized" characters and their realities. Eric Bentley maintains the bestiary metaphor by calling them "lower animals in human costume."[4] Each male, in his turn, deserves a simple label to indicate Wedekind's intent at characterization, which is as remote from real life as is the language which is spoken. Wedekind at his most aggressive in inventing a language so completely rootless, a mode of communication which Walter Sokel describes as "never heard in actual life and yet remarkably expressive of the alienation, confusion, and hysteria characteristic of modern life."[5] The dialogue is an explosive mixture of epigram, lyricism, and banality, delivered by people in asides, simultaneous speech, past one another, so that language is finally reduced to a kind of surrealistic stream-of-consciousness.

However, it is once again in terms of Freud that Wedekind's design comes most clearly into focus. In his philosophical inquiry into Freud, Herbert Marcuse defines in Freudian terms the characteristic dichotomy which is fundamental to the conflict between Lulu and established civilization. She is the representation of the *pleasure principle* (immediate satisfaction, pleasure, joy, receptiveness, absence of repression).[6] At the opposite pole is the *reality principle* of Dr. Schön: delayed satisfaction, restraint of pleasure, toil, productiveness, security. According to Freud, civilization, in its need to survive, rejects the pleasure principle and the accompanying sexual activities in order to provide opportunity for the essential activity of life: work which is productive.[7]

The bulwark of the reality principle is the father, who guarantees stability and order; but the woman is constantly a threat to this organization. "Through her sexual power, woman is dangerous to the community, the social structure of which rests on the fear displaced to the father. The development of the paternal domination into an increasingly powerful state system administered by man is thus a continuance of the primal repression which has as its purpose the even wider exclusion of woman."[8] In effect, civilization defends itself against Lulu, because she represents freedom, the reduction of repression which, according to Freud, would undermine the structure of a society based on repression. What does this society try to do with the uninhibited instrument of pleasure in its midst? It attempts to domesticate or repudiate it; to dignify it by love, or, as is the case in *Die Büchse der Pandora* to destroy it. Thus, in *Erdgeist,* the gratification of the sexual instinct is locked in a titanic struggle with civilized morality which must ultimately end with the annihilation of one or the other. For the time being, Lulu is victorious, but Wedekind further developed this thesis; and while not altering the nature of the fight, he changed the outcome.

## II   Die Büchse der Pandora

In this, the second of the "Lulu plays," "the quasi-mythic vessel of Eros," as Sokel calls Lulu, is confronted by a moral force organized and committed to her destruction. She goes on the defensive, is hunted down, caught, and destroyed by society's henchman, a perverse human being who is a repressed society's counterbalance to Lulu's "humanistic eroticism"—Jack the Ripper.[9]

The action begins in the same room where Schön had died. Lulu has been sentenced to nine years in prison for the murder, but Countess Geschwitz conceives of a fantastic plan to free her. She volunteers as a nurse for cholera victims, steals their undergarments and, wearing the infected clothing, visits Lulu in prison. They exchange underwear, and when both become ill, they are placed together in the isolation ward of the hospital. There Geschwitz masterfully disguises herself as Lulu, thus enabling her friend to escape. Lulu flees with Alwa to Paris, where she lives as the Countess Adelaide d'Oybra. But now she is unable to act freely. She becomes the hunted animal, no longer the hunter. Her enemies are a series of men who threaten to betray her to the police. Casti-Piani, a police spy in addition to being a professional procurer, wants to sell her to a high-class bordello in Cairo. Rodrigo Quast wants money. In despair Lulu turns to Schigolch, who has been living off Lulu like

the others, but comes to her assistance to help her avoid the traps
around her. The police arrive, having been informed of Lulu's where-
abouts by Casti-Piani; but, along with Alwa, Schigolch, and Geschwitz she manages to escape to London.

The last act of the play can safely be described as one of the most
sordid and grotesque in all of dramatic literature. In a miserable
Soho attic, with all of their money gone, the four individuals manage
to earn enough for daily sustenance by sending Lulu out onto the
streets as a common prostitute. As Lulu leaves on her nightly rounds,
Alwa sits in a stupor, dreaming of his past glories. His only memento
is the portrait of Lulu, which Geschwitz carries with her everywhere.
Lulu returns with her first "customer," Herr Hunedei, "a man of
gigantic stature with a clean-shaven rosy face, shy blue eyes and a
friendly smile. He is wearing a cape and a top hat." Hunedei is a
remnant from Wedekind's pantomimes, a mute who speaks only
through fantastic gestures:

Lulu: I hope you are going to give me something.
Herr Hunedei (*Holds her mouth shut and presses a gold piece into her
hand.*)
Lulu (*Inspects the gold piece and tosses it from one hand to the other.*)
Herr Hunedei (*Gives her an uncertain, questioning look.*)
Lulu: Oh, well, it's all right. (*Puts the money in her pocket.*)
Herr Hunedei (*Holds her mouth shut, gives her a few pieces of silver and
looks at her imperiously.*)
Lulu: Oh, that is good of you!
Herr Hunedei (*Leaps madly about the room, waves his arms in the air,
gazes despairingly at the ceiling.*)
Lulu (*Approaches him cautiously, puts her arm around him and kisses
him on the mouth.*)
Herr Hunedei (*Laughing soundlessly, frees himself from her and looks
enquiringly about him.*)
Lulu (*Takes the lamp from the flower stand and opens the door into her
chamber.*)
Herr Hunedei (*Goes in with a smile, raising his hat in the doorway.*)
(III, 177-79)

After Lulu leads her silent partner into her room, Alwa and Schigolch go through Hunedei's cape, searching for money. Lulu and
Hunedei soon emerge, and the macabre, silent love-making ends as
the giant noiselessly leaves the garret, with Alwa and Schigolch
hiding in the closet, so as not to interfere with the business transaction. Schigolch and Alwa indulge in considerable light-hearted

banter while waiting for Lulu's next visitor; but as they hear the footsteps approaching, in Wedekind's typical slapstick fashion, they dash for cover, Alwa beneath a rug and Schigolch in a cubbyhole, muttering: "Noblesse oblige! A decent man acts as becomes his station in life." (III, 185)

Lulu returns with an even more bizarre and exotic individual, one Kungu Poti, Crown Prince of Uahubee, in Africa. As is her custom, she asks for payment in advance, but the giant African hesitates, and Alwa charges him in a rage. But Kungu Poti smashes him to the floor, and Schigolch drags the mortally wounded Alwa into Lulu's bedroom. The Prince has left the garret, with Lulu right behind him, soon to be followed by Schigolch, in search of a drink. Lulu's next pickup is for pure comic relief; she appears with the Swiss "Privatdozent" Hilti, a timid and frightened academician:

Lulu (gaily): Come in, come in! You'll stay the night with me?
Dr. Hilti: But I have no more than five shillings on me. I never take more when I go out.
Lulu: That's enough because it's you. You have such honest eyes!—Come, give me a kiss!
Dr. Hilti: Jesus, Mary, Joseph. . .
Lulu: Please, Please, be quiet!
Dr. Hilti: But devil take it, it's the first time I've ever been with a woman.
Lulu: Are you married?
Dr. Hilti: For God's sake! What makes you think I'm married? No. I'm a lecturer; I teach philosophy at the University. By God, I come of one of the best families of Basel; as a student I used to get only two francs' pocket money, and I had better uses for it than women. (III, 188)

Hilti's expedition to Soho was forced upon him by his lack of experience in matters of love. Lulu, now in the capacity of the experienced mistress of love, is to act as educator:

Dr. Hilti: But now I need it. I got engaged this evening to a girl from one of Basel's oldest families.
Lulu: Is your fiancée pretty?
Dr. Hilti: Yes, she has two million.—I tell you, I can hardly wait to see what it's like. (III, 189)

Even in this cameo appearance of an academician Wedekind could not resist criticism. Hilti is a twofold predator, both financial and sexual.

Hilti's exit is even more precipitous than Kungu Poti's, and more grotesque, framed as it is between the actual death of Alwa and the attempted suicide of Geschwitz:

(*Lulu conducts Dr. Hilti into her chamber.*)
Geschwitz (*Pulls a small black revolver out of her pocket and holds it to her forehead*): Come, come . . . beloved!
Dr. Hilti (*Snatches the door open from within and rushes out*): What sort of dirty business is this!—There's a body in there!
Lulu (*The lamp in her hand, holds him by the sleeve*): Stay with me!
Dr. Hilti: A dead body! A corpse!
Lulu: Stay with me! Stay with me!
Dr. Hilti: There's a corpse lying in there in—a dirty business, by God! How does one get out of here? (*Catching sight of Geschwitz.*) And there is the devil! Dirty business, dirty business—My God! (*Exit.*)
Lulu: Stop!—Stop! (*Rushes after him.*) (III, 189)

Geschwitz, left alone for the moment, now decides on hanging herself, but the cord around her neck breaks, leaving her sprawled on the floor clutching Lulu's portrait. Countess Geschwitz, whom Wedekind conceived of as the most tragic figure of *Pandora*, is the most incomprehensible creature in the play.[10] One feels a genuine compassion for her state; and her love for Lulu is the only tangible thing that is consistent. Yet Wedekind makes her attempted suicides ludicrous, although she awakens the only real sense of pathos—ridiculous as she may seem with a broken rope around her neck—as she cries out: "My adored angel! My beloved! My star! Have pity on me, have pity on me, have pity on me!"

It is at this very moment that Lulu once again returns, unknowingly, with Jack the Ripper. After having visited with Lulu, he takes back his money, along with some of hers, before he consents to remain with her. They go off into the bedroom, leaving Geschwitz alone once again to soliloquize: "This is the last evening I shall spend with these people. I shall go back to Germany. My mother will send me money for the fare. I shall take my matriculation. I must fight for women's rights, study jurisprudence." Suddenly Lulu runs screaming from the room, chased by the sex maniac, bent over like some sort of monstrous animal. Geschwitz pulls out her revolver, but before she can shoot him Jack plunges a knife into her stomach and drags Lulu back into the room. For a frightening moment the stage is empty except for the dying countess. Soon Jack returns, washes

Lulu's blood from his hands, and leaves after drying them on Gesch-witz' petticoat.

In *Pandora* Lulu has come to an end which she herself had envi-sioned, as she acknowledges in the first act: "Every few nights I used to dream that I'd fallen into the hands of a sex maniac." As she acts out her mythic role as the inevitable victim of a civilization determined to destroy her, Lulu anticipates her end fatalistically. But this does make her death less pathetic, because Wedekind ex-tends his allegorical treatment of the innocent and freedom-seeking creature to the miserable Soho flat, where society inflicts its perfect revenge on her. First, she is degraded. As a prostitute, she is untrue to her very nature. "I can't make love on command," she laments. For her, prostitution is the lowest form of existence.[11] "Is there any-thing sadder in this world than a street-walker?" The strength which she so magnificently demonstrated in *Erdgeist* is gone, and she is left completely disarmed before Jack, her opposite number, but a prod-uct of "the general perversion of the human existence in a repressive culture," a horrible sexual variant of inhibited humanity.[12] But now Lulu is no match. She is a common whore, and as such she is annihilated.

### III  *Lulu's Heritage*

In 1938, Antonin Artaud, the most penetrating spokesman for the theater of revolt, wrote as follows in *The Theatre and Its Double:*

This true freedom is dark, and infallibly identified with sexual freedom which is also dark. . . And that is why the great Myths are dark, so that one cannot imagine, save in the atmosphere of carnage, torture, and blood-shed all the magnificent Fables which recount to the multitudes the first sexual division and the first carnage of essences that appeared in creation.[13]

The "true freedom" in the theater which Artaud was promulgating would seem to have been anticipated by Wedekind's dark myth of Lulu almost half a century earlier. Robert Brustein identifies Artaud's thesis that "the archetypal, pre-logical, primitive spirit still lives in the unconscious of Western man, though deeply submerged under the dead skin of civilization. For it is linked to the sexual instinct itself."[14] Brustein's judgment is strikingly relevant when applied to the conflict between Lulu and society. It, too, is the conflict of a primitive force, the Earth-Spirit, with the authoritarian traditions of a patriarchal Christianity whose order is threatened by the alien intruder. Wedekind, like Artaud, saw beauty in Lulu's destruction of the symbols of this society which is perverse. Her "cruelty" is the essential means by which humanity must be purged of its acquired repression. Wedekind's Lulu plays urge a return to the primal "time of evil" when mankind existed without memory or consciousness. Lulu herself is the first of the representatives of the anti-social, destructive forces which dramatists from Brecht to the present have forced on a contented civilization.

But if Lulu was given particular meaning by the avant-garde theater in resurrecting her as a modern-day symbol for its archetypal vision, she attained her immortality elsewhere. It was through the medium of the motion picture that Lulu found her fullest expression in the twentieth century. Starting with the pre-World War I years and reaching a peak during the Weimar Republic, a host of female "vamps" paraded across the motion picture screen, a highly marketable popularization of Lulu, changed from the innocent and pristine figure created by Wedekind to the man-eater, a "kiss-me-you-fool" love goddess who specialized in devouring simple middle-class burghers.[15]

A legion of actresses made a career out of this role, which became a fixture in screen scenarios. *Die Büchse der Pandora* itself was made into a film in 1929—along with *Frühlings Erwachen*, which likewise spawned a whole school of "juvenile insurgence" films.[16] The most celebrated "Lulu-Gestalt" in motion picture history was actually somewhat less Wedekind-inspired. In 1905 Heinrich Mann, the younger of the two famous brothers, wrote a bitingly satirical novel about the German middle class, *Professor Unrat*. In it he created a scarcely concealed imitation of Wedekind's arch female in Lola Lola, who manipulates and finally destroys a pompous, middle-aged high school professor.[17] It was Marlene Dietrich who portrayed Lola in the film version, *Der blaue Engel*, which appeared in 1930. Her performance of the heartless seductress epitomized the metamorphosis which Wedekind's Lulu had undergone. From the representation of mankind's subconscious fear of uninhibited freedom, she turned into a vain, petty bourgeois tart.

# CHAPTER 7

# *Lamentations*

"Put yourself in my place, as I introduce myself to the Berlin public as a buffoon and clown, while my lips are not permitted to utter the best, the holiest things which I as a serious man have to say."
Wedekind

A S the nineteenth century drew to a close, Frank Wedekind could look back on a career that at best can be called undistinguished. His plays were not being produced or read, and whatever reputation he enjoyed resulted from his witty essays and cartoon captions in *Simplizissimus*. More and more he began to view himself as a tragic figure, an oppressed artist victimized by a cruel, smugly ignorant society, as what Sokel has called the "poeta dolorosus."[1] Stigmatized by the censor, ignored by the public, Wedekind turned to his writing to complain, and he produced a series of strikingly autobiographical works which primarily lament the fate of the misunderstood artist.

I

*"I must do what is demanded of me, because I am obligated by contract. Every breath that I have belongs to the public."*
Gerardo in *Der Kammersänger*

Wedekind represents two sides of the artist's mentality in the first of his confessional dramas, *Der Kammersänger* (*The Tenor*, 1897), a one-act play which ultimately became the most performed of his dramatic works as well as a standard anthology piece. One aspect of the artist is depicted by Gerardo, an internationally known tenor, who is rushing to catch his train for Brussels to sing the role of Tristan in Wagner's opera. Wedekind himself described Gerardo as "a brutal intelligence, a blown-up Philistine soul," but one who is trapped and

*[ 80 ]*

controlled by an adoring public. Yet he considers himself the epitome
of artistic success, the object of nightly applause. This adoration
becomes somewhat of a burden for Gerardo. As he rehearses in the
few moments left before his taxi arrives, he discovers a lovesick
teen-ager hiding behind the curtains of his hotel room.

Miss Coeurne (*Speaks with an English accent*): I was just bringing you
these roses, and—
Gerardo: And—and what?
Miss Coeurne: And myself!—I don't know whether you understand me?
(III, 207)

Gerardo understands her all too well and manages to satisfy the
young lady with an autographed picture of himself.

Gerardo continues the impromptu rehearsal as his luggage receives
final attention, but once again is interrupted, this time by an aged
composer, Professor Dühring, who has spent his entire life in devo-
tion to his art, but has never had one single work performed or
published. At seventy, Dühring remains in every fiber of his being
the artist who will not bend to the public's desires. A proud, lonely
man, he comes now to Gerardo to beg, to expose himself to his most
complete humiliation:

Dühring: Maestro—I have—I have an opera.
Gerardo: How did you get in?
Dühring: I have been waiting for two hours for a chance to run up the
stairs without being seen.
Gerardo: I don't have time. My train leaves in forty minutes.
Dühring: You don't have time! What should I say? You are thirty and a
great success. You have your whole life before you. Just listen to your
part in my opera. You promised me you'd listen to it when you came
to this city. (III, 214)

Gerardo reacts with boredom, impatience, then finally with disgust
and anger about a life having been wasted in the futile hope for
recognition:

Gerardo: What have you done with your life? You have wasted it shame-
fully.
Dühring: To me art is the highest concept in the world!
Gerardo: This may be the belief of people such as you, who are genuinely
interested in making this point of view a reality. But nobody else
believes it! We artists are no more than a luxury article for the use

of the bourgeoisie. . . They notice us as little as they notice the air that separates them from the stage. *That's the meaning of the commodity you call art!* That's what you have sacrificed fifty years of your life for! (III, 224)

When Gerardo, out of pity, offers the old man money, this proves too much for poor Dühring, who exits in a pathetic state of agitation, as the exhausted and uncomprehending Gerardo sinks down into a chair, muttering: "Pleased to have met you."

But even as he sits, there is another interruption. Helena Marowa, a woman "of blinding beauty, twenty years old," pushes her way past the valet. She threatens Gerardo: either take her with him, or she will kill herself. Helena cannot allow herself to be parted from the singer and is willing to sacrifice everything she has: husband, children, social position. But Gerardo does not even permit himself to be tempted:

Gerardo: I can't take you with me, dearest, because my contract forbids me to marry, or even to travel in the company of ladies.
Helena (*perplexed*): Who can forbid such a thing!
Gerardo: My contract. (III, 229)

Helena, true to her word, aims a pistol at herself and shoots. Now Gerardo is really in a bind. Obviously concerned about her condition, but still desperate to catch his train, he frantically dashes about the room in an effort to organize his emotions and his luggage:

Gerardo (*Jumping up and down, runs to the door and collides with the hotel manager*): Send for the police! I must be arrested! If I leave, I'm a monster, and if I stay, I'm in for breach of contract, I'm ruined! I still have (*looking at his watch*) a minute and ten seconds. Quick, I've got to be arrested before then—And my trunks? Is the carriage at the door?
Manager: It has been waiting twenty minutes, Mr. Gerardo.
Gerardo (*Bending over her*): Helena! (*to himself*) Well, after all—(*to the manager*) Have you called the doctor?
Manager: Yes, we had the doctor called at once. He will be here any minute.
Gerardo (*Holding her in his arms*): Helena! Don't you know me any more? Helena! The doctor will be here right away, Helena. This is your Oscar.
Bellboy (*at center door*): Can't find any policeman, sir.
Gerardo (*Lets Helena's body drop back*): Well, if I can't get arrested,

that settles it. I must catch the train and sing *Tristan* in Brussels
tomorrow night. (*Gathers up his music and exits, bumping into several chairs.*) (III, 240)

Above all, *Der Kammersänger* is dominated by a sense of furious
tempo. Wedekind built into the plot an urgency and speed which
is characterized by Gerardo's constant refrain: "I must sing *Tristan*
in Brussels tomorrow!" The action starts in high gear and accelerates
from there, until the general agitation transforms the play into a
kind of Mack Sennett, high-speed two-reeler. Actually, there is a
strong suggestion that Wedekind was aware of the similarity with
some of the slapstick movie "bits" encountered in the earliest silent
films. An instance of this occurs while Dühring, at his most moving
moment, pleads with Gerardo while the singer distractedly taps his
fingers on the marble fireplace. As the old man talks, Gerardo's
attention is caught by something behind the fixture. He reaches
behind and pulls out someone whom the stage direction describes
simply as a female piano teacher, another of the singer's host of
admirers. Dühring continues his long-winded speech as Gerardo
drags the lady across the room and out the door, then nonchalantly
turns to the composer simply to say, "Please, do continue!" This
spirit of grotesque high-jinx comes through just as strongly in the
episodes with the childish admirer Miss Coeurne and the elegant
Helena Marowa.

But it is the central issue, between Gerardo and Dühring, which
represents Wedekind's direct confrontation with himself. On the
surface, it appears as if the author had loaded the deck in favor
of Dühring (Wedekind?), the genius who must suffer society's
monumental lack of interest, while the lesser creative spirits, the
mere performers, win accolades. Gerardo offers the cynical view:
"There are no undiscovered geniuses," he shouts in anger. Gerardo
also loses stature because he allows himself to be stripped of his
independence. Like all of Wedekind's protagonists, he views himself
in terms of an animal existence: "The chains on me are more tightly
drawn than the harness of a carriage horse. . . . Don't demand the
slightest expression of *personal freedom* from me; that's too much
to demand of a slave, which is what I am." He detests Dühring for
having the temerity to attempt to exercise his freedom of choice.
"Man is born a slave" and must adapt himself as best as possible to
the society in which he has to function.

But Wedekind's sense of irony is too highly developed to make the Gerardo-Dühring conflict a black-and-white confrontation of artless cynicism and artistic idealism. His self-pity does not go so far as make the ancient professor his symbol of righteous defiance, the truly great artist scorned by society. For Dühring is *not* a genius, or at least Wedekind prefers not to take him too seriously. When he finally manages to get to Gerardo's piano, Dühring produces some incredible effects. He loses his place, has a wretched voice which he uses to sing all the roles, including a falsetto for the female part, and produces what Wedekind describes as a "chaotic orchestration." Rather ruthlessly, Dühring's inner legitimacy is taken away from him by Wedekind; and his "feverish torment" is meant to appear ridiculous.[2] Wedekind's reference to his own artistic merit is not the only instance of sardonic irony which we encounter in this group of plays which are intended to define the cleavage between artist and audience.

## II  Der Marquis von Keith

In *Der Kammersänger* Wedekind explored the relationship of the artist to his public by contrasting the values of two men. Having found the formula, he plays with variations of it in *Der Marquis von Keith* (1900). Wedekind expands the subject to include a personal dichotomy which troubled him a great deal, judging from the elaborate Wedekind-Hauptmann paradigm which was shown earlier. In *Keith* Wedekind goes in for some fairly extensive self-analysis in exploring what he considered the two souls within himself: the amoral, detached artist living outside of society, and the committed moralist who wants to improve it. From all indications, Wedekind, at this time of his life, saw himself in the role of the amoralist, but there always gnawed deep inside him the thought that he would be happiest living within a society that could accept him.[3]

Keith himself is a picaresque hero, a philosopher–horse-thief whom Wedekind describes as "a Don Quixote of life's pleasures." He is a climber who wants possession of everything from which he is excluded. His origins are common, as is his appearance. He limps, and his elegant gloves cannot hide the course roughness of his skin. "Keith" is an assumed name, taken in order to gain access to a society which wants no part of him.

Ernst Scholz, on the other hand, is "a Don Quixote of morality." Born Graf Trautenau, he renounces his title in order to move closer to the mass of humanity. But his altruism is misled, for while working as an overzealous railroad official he was responsible for the death of twenty people in a terrible accident. In a final effort at repentance, Scholz, the moralist who suffers from a bad conscience, turns himself over to his childhood friend, now named von Keith (who has no conscience at all) in the hopes of finding a meaning in life. Scholz enters Keith's life at a time when his friend is testing all the elasticity at his disposal, in an effort to attain the pinnacle of financial and social success. The scene is Munich in the year 1899, where Keith is involved in a grand design to build a colossal entertainment hall. Completely without any financial resources of his own, he never worries about his ability to find people willing to support him, and for a time he manages magnificently. Keith has no fear of life, and his only real asset, his will to triumph, gives him the edge over society.

But his elaborate venture in the entertainment business stretches even Keith's abilities. At home he is living with a simple middle-class girl named Molly, who is contented to have Keith remain a failure, knowing that with his success will come the end of their relationship. Meanwhile, Keith has found two solid Munich businessmen who are willing to give him complete financial support, provided that Keith can also deliver assurances that Consul Casimir, the city's most prestigious investor, will also participate. Naturally Keith guarantees Casimir's investment, although no such transaction has taken place. Keith is convinced that Casimir can be persuaded to join his organization. His trump is the Countess Werdenfels, a greatly admired international beauty, whom Keith intends to bill as his star attraction at the gala opening. Just as matters seem to go smoothly for Keith, his world suddenly collapses. He meets his match in Casimir, who possesses all of Keith's ruthlessness and elasticity, as well as vast amounts of money. Casimir realizes that he has Keith in a bind and deftly withholds his support of the project until the crucial moment, when he withdraws completely, leaving Keith open to charges of fraud. When the other investors discover that Keith is not even keeping books of the financial operations, they take the control of the corporation away from him. Casimir proposes marriage to the countess, and she too abandons Keith. Meanwhile Molly, seeing her lover about to attain his goals, drowns herself in the Isar River.

But Keith refuses to give up. He still has one friend, his "pupil" Scholz, who has been observing, even participating in, the extraordinary events. He has had his exposure to the world of "humanity" and has found it not to his taste. As Anna leaves Keith to join Casimir, Scholz enters, and in a confrontation which Thomas Mann called the most harrowing he has ever experienced, Keith begs for money to save his crumbling empire.[4] For Scholz, there is no pleasure in life, and he would spare his friend the bother of searching for it:

Scholz: I am firmly convinced that the best thing for you is to accompany me.
Keith: Where to?
Scholz: To a private sanatorium.
Keith: Give me thirty thousand marks and I'll come along.
Scholz: If you accompany me you will not need any more money. You'll find a more comfortable life than you've ever known. We'll keep a horse and carriage, play billiards—
Keith: Give me thirty thousand marks!! Do you want me to grovel before you? I can be arrested on the spot!
Scholz: Have things gone so far? I don't give sums like that to a madman!
Keith: You're the madman!
Scholz: I have come to my senses.
Keith: If you want to go into a lunatic asylum because you've come to your senses—go right ahead! (IV, 94)

To escape from the madness of the world, Scholz elects to enter a madhouse, leaving Keith to face a hostile crowd of eyewitnesses to Molly's death. Casimir intervenes and quiets the mob, gives Keith ten thousand marks and instructs him to leave town.

Keith must decide whether to leave Munich or to admit his failure and take a step as drastic, or even more drastic, than Scholz. Keith is left alone, with Casimir's money in one hand and a revolver in the other:

Keith (*The revolver in his left hand, the money in his right, takes several steps toward the couch but shrinks back in horror. Then he irresolutely looks at the revolver and the money in turn. As he lays the revolver behind him on the center table, with a grin*): Life is a roller coaster. . .
(IV, 98)

(*curtain*)

Keith makes his choice; he decides to live and, reasserting his code of ethics, rejects Scholz's own brand of renunciation as well. He will continue to play the knave at the expense of the fools. Keith's belief in himself is restored; and as the curtain falls, his determination to make society crawl at his knees is no less convincing. The "Tatmensch" is still a man of action.

Wedekind leaves no doubt where his sympathy lies. Keith stands out against a background of boorish high financiers and pseudo-artists. The businessmen of Munich are predatory stereotypes, greedy and hungry for money, but without Keith's scintillating wit and imagination. Keith's entourage includes the perpetually downcast writer Sommersberg, author of *Songs of a Happy Man,* hopeless and ridiculous in his quest for fame; also, there is Saranieff—"wearing a frock coat with sleeves a little too short, thick shoes, and bright red gloves"—who passionately idealizes art while making his living as a forger. Almost as an afterthought, Wedekind introduces Käthi, a one-dimensional "Lulu-figure," whom the group names Simba because she emits an exciting animalism.

But what really separates Keith from the herd is his wit. Keith's language is breathtakingly concentrated, and it is not surprising that a volume of aphorisms from *Der Marquis von Keith* appeared as an independent publication.[5] Keith is Wedekind's most quotable creation by far, and the sharpness of his mind is applied completely to articulating the philosophy of life which has guided him:

I expect to reach the point some day where the mixture of philosopher and horse-thief will be fully appreciated. . . Truth is our most precious possession and we must use it sparingly. . . For the true artist the mind is a hindrance. . . You can't impress a dog with fireworks, but the most rational man feels hurt if you don't give him any. . . The most modern is always the cheapest and the most effective. . . The world is a cursedly sly beast, not easily conquered. But once you succeed, you are proof against any misfortune. . . Any ass can suffer misfortune; it takes skill to exploit it to one's advantage. . . I have not suffered self-denial thousands of times in my life in order to do what people usually do. . . No hour of my existence is bearable unless it brings me closer to my goal. . . I have asked no one for my existence, and from that I deduce that I'm justified in living as I please. . . *Morality* is the best business in the world. . . Thank God, I have never doubted that I am different from other men![6]

In *Der Marquis von Keith,* Wedekind took a long, hard look at his own life. Although there is no specific resemblance to Keith (the actual model for the latter was Wedekind's close friend Willi Gretor), his struggle was also Wedekind's. The problem which Wedekind solved for himself in *Keith* is that of the choice between alternatives: renunciation in the face of defeat or continuation of the struggle, although the world considers you an outsider. Keith, with "his coarse red hands of a clown" and his limp, mocked by society and scorned as a rogue, laughs and goes on. His decision *to continue* the struggle was also Wedekind's.

FRANK WEDEKIND

### III  König Nicolo, oder So ist das Leben

Between the writing of *Keith* and his next play, *König Nicolo,*
Wedekind served his jail sentence for "Majestätsbeleidigung." The
impact of that experience was most significant for him; given the
particular autobiographical bent of the two previous plays, Wedekind's reaction to what he considered a monumental travesty of
justice was naturally channeled into *König Nicolo.* The energetic
tone of *Der Kammersänger* and *Keith* gives way to an uncharacter-
istically elegiac mood, one that borders on self-pity, as Wedekind
moves closer and closer to a more complete identification with the
protagonist. The precariousness of the artist's life was accompanied
by much good fun in the previous plays; but in *König Nicolo* Wedekind puts everything in the desired perspective when the very first
lines are uttered by the king: "Please, no laughter!" (IV, 105)

Also unusual for Wedekind was the setting for the play, the Italy
of the Renaissance. Nicolo is King of Umbria and rules from his
palace in Perugia. He is far from being an ideal monarch and dis-
sipates the royal treasury with elaborate masked balls and entertainments. Finally, the overtaxed masses rebel and overthrow the vain
ruler. A republic, led by the town's master butcher, Pietro Folchi, is
established. When Nicolo arrogantly asserts his inherited rights of
kingship, the new government banishes him and his daughter Alma
from Umbria, upon pain of death should they be found within the
borders of the country. As they are being escorted to the border,
Nicolo and Alma escape from their guards and throw themselves
into the river, where they are believed drowned.

Having been declared officially dead, Nicolo and Alma wander
undetected through his former domains, seeking any sort of employ-
ment to keep themselves alive. His first plebeian position is as
apprentice to the tailor Pandulfo in Padua. He becomes very popular
with the town ladies, while Alma, disguised as a young boy, works
for the town clerk. Because of his success with the customers, Nicolo
is terribly abused by the jealous apprentices in the shop who resent
his success; but he cannot lower himself to their level. It would be
beneath his dignity. He berates himself for retaining his royal nature:
"Oh curse the king who keeps me from smashing these wretches!
A curse upon him who keeps me from being a human being like any
other!" (IV, 128)

The apprentices, overhearing Nicolo, are outraged at what they
consider an insult to their beloved new ruler, and after giving him
a thorough beating, drag Nicolo off to court, where he is convicted

of "Majestätsbeleidigung." In a bitterly grotesque trial which, no doubt, reflected Wedekind's image of his own courtroom experience regarding the same charge, the former king is convicted, sentenced to two years' imprisonment, and once again banished for life from the province.

Nicolo views the two years in jail as a respite from a mad world he is learning to understand. After his release, he and Alma, still disguised as a youth, wander through the countryside to witness the dedication of the new royal church, which is also the gathering place for a gigantic audition of entertainers of all sorts looking for engagements. The tryouts take place beneath a gallows late at night, and in an atmosphere which Fechter describes as "a fantastic Walpurgisnight," the auditions begin. Nicolo decides that he will use the occasion to make his confession to the world and reveal his true identity. When he is asked to audition, he mounts a rock and declaims:

> I am the royal ruler of this land,
> God's chosen own, but recognized by none.
> (IV, 149)

Nicolo is deadly serious, but his solemnity is met by hilarious laughter. Amidst cries of "Da capo! Da capo!" he tries eloquently to explain the earnestness of his revelation: "My subject on the stage is one of high tragedy!" But again the reaction is one of uproarious laughter and applause. He is acknowledged as the greatest comedian among them. The numerous producers, seeing his tremendous success, compete with one another for Nicolo's services. One of them succeeds in engaging his talents, and Alma is hired as an assistant. The former king leaves as Epaminondas Alexandrion, a royal clown.

Nicolo proves to be a sensational attraction everywhere, finally being invited to a command performance before the new king, Pietro. Once again he speaks his regal lines, and while the people applaud in delight, Pietro is moved by the wisdom of Nicolo's speech about the passing of all things and the vanity of man. Impressed by the actor's wisdom as well as his mock heroic humor, Pietro decides to keep him at court—and Nicolo is engaged as personal jester to the king.

Nicolo has returned to his throne—as a fool. Matters are complicated when the crown prince Filippo falls in love with Alma, who has thrown off her disguise, and when Pietro orders his fool to forbid his daughter to see Filippo, Nicolo, true to his role, haughtily informs him that his is not the power to forbid. For this outburst, Pietro angrily banishes his jester from the kingdom, but the irony of this oft-repeated judgment is too much for Nicolo, and he informs the king of the previous banishments, also admitting that he is King Nicolo, the former ruler of Umbria. The court and king react with shock and sadness, believing that the jester has really gone mad. Pietro tries to convince him that the real Nicolo has drowned many years ago. The frustration overwhelms Nicolo. Unable to prove his identity, he staggers toward the throne: "Who can possibly prove by means of his corpse that he is actually a king!—Too late—too late! —Such is life." (IV, 180) He dies, a clown trying to play the king to the end. But Alma appears to verify her father's story, to the horror of Pietro. He orders Nicolo to be buried secretly in the royal crypt: "I don't want it said of me that I made a king my court jester." In death Nicolo gains at least in part the recognition he was unable to attain in life.

Although Wedekind made an effort to detach himself from the play by setting it in a fairytale atmosphere of fifteenth-century Italy, the work is baldly, often uncomfortably, autobiographical. One need only substitute "Dichter" for "König" to recognize Wedekind's personal lament over his own artistic situation. Through the mouth of the outcast, unrecognized king, the author expresses all of his own bitter complaints. Yet Wedekind for the most part avoids wallowing in a self-pity which would have destroyed the play. He never permits himself to escape his own irony, and the initial characterization of Nicolo is distinctly unsympathetic. The king is vain and egotistical, while the upstart butcher, with *his* warm sensitivity, stands in sharp contrast. Even as Nicolo grows in stature, the dramatic irony continues to undercut him. He wins his first laurels not as a king, but as a ladies' tailor.

Where Wedekind comes into closest contact with Nicolo—in the trial scene and the tragic-figure-as-clown episodes—the king's martyrdom is unavoidably his own, and any theatergoer seeing the play in Wedekind's lifetime could not have missed the point. There is no doubt that there is a certain datedness to *König Nicolo*, since Wedekind conceived of the pivotal parts of the plot as a type of contemporary comment on the injustices done to him. In fact, Nicolo's defense is remarkably similar to the one which Wedekind mounted at his own trial; namely that it was beneath the dignity of a monarch to allow himself to feel insulted by a subject. Even the audience reaction to Nicolo's acting registers most graphically when considered along with public reaction to Wedekind's efforts to act in his own plays.[7]

*König Nicolo* is a typical "artist's drama." The tragic idea of the play is the artist's alienation from his public and the total misconception of the public in comprehending artistic truth. For Wedekind, *König Nicolo* had a particular meaning, but as Sokel points out, it had an even greater significance to the entire generation of writers immediately following Wedekind.[8] The conflict, for them as for Nicolo, was one between the free spirit and society, which greeted the serious poet with laughter.[9] The public wanted entertainment, not messianic visions. German writers such as Hanns Johst, Georg Kaiser, and Georg Trakl shared Wedekind's sense of the isolated artist fighting for recognition from a smug majority who remained indifferent to his lament.

Wedekind naturally frames this conflict in his own unique fashion. He still has a fundamentally aggressive attitude toward society not only as a passive, but also as a destructive force. The people do more than ignore Nicolo; they also try to destroy him. Once again the struggle becomes one of "the predatory animals" hunting down "the beautiful, wild animal." As Nicolo gradually withdraws from the world, he finds the company of men less and less desirable and prefers to spend his time with the kind animals of the field. But society is not content to let him escape; he must be sought out and killed. The prosecuting attorney's remarks at his second trial defines society's attitude toward Nicolo: "Such a wild animal, because of his baseness as well as the threat he poses to all of society, deserves no fate other than death, so that no trace might remain of him on this earth." (IV, 135) The tailor's offence is magnified to a mortal crime. The outsider, the individual of noble spirit, is a threat that must be destroyed. For a time, Nicolo considers the possibility of adjusting, and even suggests to Alma that she "howl with the wolves": "You are the lamb among the wolves, who, for the time being, have sworn to protect you against harm. But wolves remain wolves! And in the end, if the lamb does not want to be torn to pieces, she too must become a wolf." (IV, 158) For Nicolo, such advice is impossible. He must remain true to his honor and integrity, even at the cost of his life.

IV   Hidalla, oder Karl Hetmann der Zwergriese

In his very next play, *Hidalla, oder Karl Hetmann der Zwergriese*

(*Karl Hetmann, the Dwarf-Giant,* 1903), Wedekind abandons the historical distance of *König Nicolo* and treats the identical theme with an eruptive savagery that at times approaches hysteria. Hetmann is, once again, the artist outside of society. This time he is a social scientist, badly crippled since birth—an extension of Keith's limp—who is advocating a new order. As secretary of "The International Society for the Propagation of Human Thoroughbreds," an organization which he founded, Hetmann hopes to create a new moral order for the world, one that is based on beauty and natural love. The constitution removes all "normal" obligations regarding family and marriage from its members, and no participant is permitted to deny the favors of love upon request. The only prerequisite for admission is physical perfection; but because of his deformity and ugliness, Hetmann does not permit himself to join. Yet, his magnetic rhetoric wins him a large number of followers.

Hetmann wants to create a race of "Übermenschen" in the best Nietzschean tradition, and taken the nature of Hetmann's statements, there is little doubt that Wedekind clearly had Nietzsche in mind: "Our new morality demands sacrifices as never before. Today the universal morality is at the service of the highest human happiness, the family. This highest form of human happiness must be sacrificed first by the members of our order." (IV, 205–6) Hetmann is referred to as "the great prophet" by those who admire him, and as a madman by his detractors. To still others, he appears as an attractive investment which promises lucrative return.

Rudolf Launhart is a successful businessman who sees in Hetmann the opportunity for a financial "kill." Like Keith, Launhart has a trenchant quip for every occasion and has little use for Hetmann other than to supply him with money: "You can make better deals with fools than with philosophers!" (IV, 204) Launhart agrees to publish Hetmann's pamphlets, which prove to be tremendously popular. However, the police confiscate one issue which contains an essay by Hetmann "Love in Middle-class Culture Compared to that of Our Domesticated Animals."

What next occurs in the play is a fascinating example of Wedekind's documentary theater: it is a literal retelling of the events preceding his own arrest. The real-life counterpart of Launhart now appears quite clearly. It is Albert Langen, Wedekind's publisher. In *Karl Hetmann* the police appear in the editorial offices, and while Launhart sits in Paris watching the sales of his publications soar because of the notoriety, Hetmann is brought to trial and convicted.

Upon his release from prison, he continues zealously to propagate the new faith: "The next battle for freedom will be directed against the feudalism of love!" he cries and embarks on a series of lectures to stir up the faithful and unfaithful alike. (IV, 238)

But his appearance on the lecture platform produces laughter in the audience, as he berates them for their moral ugliness—he, the embodiment of ugliness, a deformed dwarf. When one of his erstwhile followers interrupts a lecture and announces to the people that Hetmann is insane, a wild riot ensues and Hetmann is beaten up. The charge of insanity is taken seriously, and Hetmann is institutionalized for observation. He emerges disenchanted, but determined to hold on to his beliefs, no longer as a teacher, but merely as a forgotten prophet.

But Hetmann has not been forgotten. He is still in demand. The director of a famous circus wants to engage him and his doctrine for the staggering sum of 500 marks an evening—if Hetmann will appear as a clown! Hetmann, after gasping in horror at the sudden discovery that to society he is no more than a fool, staggers out of the room and hangs himself.

There are several obvious motifs which form interesting connections between *Karl Hetmann* and the previous plays of this period. Keith, Nicolo, and Hetmann are each accused of being insane, and both Keith and Hetmann are intimately involved with asylums.[10] All three protagonists also assume the image of a clown for at least a portion of each play, and for Nicolo and Hetmann the assumption of this role magnifies their tragic existence. Hetmann himself is most like the aged composer Dühring in *Der Kammersänger*, with his unbending dedication to his cause, even if it means the curse of ridicule.

Of all of the Wedekind-like heroes of these personal plays, Hetmann seems the most identifiable with the author. His philosophical and social cause is an echo of much of what Wedekind had espoused in the earlier works. They share a dislike of the women's emancipation movement, an intensive belief in the morality of physical beauty, and an aggressive rejection of the modern world's sexual attitudes. But again Wedekind did not hesitate to undercut his hero—and himself. The malformed and toothless little prophet is a pitiful human specimen, and his exaggerated combativeness excludes any practical acceptance of his credo. But the ultimate irony is that his relationship to his code must remain theoretical and never actual, since his ugliness also excludes him from participation. If Wedekind considered himself a prophet, he was not blind to the uselessness of prophesying to an age which refused to listen, or worse still, mocked him.

It seems also likely that Wedekind had still another unappreciated prophet in mind when he created Hetmann. The resemblance between Hetmann's visionary pronouncements and those of Friedrich Nietzsche are striking, as are the mutual fates of the two philosophers. Nietzsche, who died in a mental institution in 1900 and who was just coming into vogue around the turn of the century, was likewise "unzeitgemäss," out of touch with his times (his first major published work was entitled *Unzeitgemässe Betrachtungen,* 1873), and had to wait for a future generation to receive more sympathetic treatment. One of Hetmann's passionate followers laments his master's fate in terms which are identifiable with the early reception of Nietzsche: "It is most regrettable that Hetmannism will have to wait decades before it receives the recognition which it deserves." (IV, 260) But here, too, Wedekind's irony makes itself felt. In his own lifetime Hetmann receives the ultimate deification which Nietzsche was just beginning to experience after his death. He is followed around by a young doctoral candidate who wants to write a learned thesis based on Hetmannism!

A notable shift in the attitude of the author affects his treatment of the high-flying businessman Launhart. In *Der Marquis von Keith,* Wedekind portrays his materialistic confidence man with a dynamic verve and pays tribute to Keith's morality of money. In Launhart, he created more or less another Keith, but makes him the villain. Keith's cynicism and unscrupulousness are no longer virtues, and Hetmann scorns Keith's materialism. If a confrontation between these two protagonists could have been arranged, one might speculate that Keith would exploit Hetmann's idealism just exactly as had Launhart. Keith was Wedekind's last sympathetic capitalist. Beginning with Launhart, he presented a series of villainous moneymakers who automatically fell into the role of the negative forces opposing the heroes.

Another aspect of the capitalist's mentality provides additional farcical material in *Karl Hetmann* and also illustrates what point Wedekind had reached in his relationship to America. Mrs. Isabel Grant, a wealthy American widow, is enchanted with Hetmann's society and would like to buy her way into it. Her money is her greatest asset, but it cannot buy her fluency in German; hers is hilariously ungrammatical: "A-oh, Mr. Hetmann, ich will Sie schenken fünfzigtausend Mark! Nicht Sie will ich schenken! Ich will schenken für die Bund zu Züchtung von die Rassenmenschen!" (IV, 217) As the organization is on the verge of collapse because of Launhart's manipulations, she literally buys Pietro Alessandro Morosini, a beautiful and brainless body, who is the most admired member of the group:

Mrs. Grant (*steigt auf den Sessel, auf dem sie vorher sass, und flüstert Morosini zu*): Ich liebe Sie mit ganze Seele, Morosini. Ich will ziegen Papiere von Einkünfte, dass ich habe zwanzigtausend Dollar in jede Jahr, das ist mein. (IV, 250)

Mrs. Grant represents the final phase of Wedekind's changing image of America. She is a vulgar, caricaturized boor who flaunts her wealth, a female capitalist with absolutely no virtues whatsoever. America disappears from the plays as a land representing hope and enlightenment, and the abstract vision is replaced with several concrete representatives—all most unflattering—of the land which earlier had held such promise for Wedekind. It is difficult to say what prompted the shift in attitude, for there was no precedence in German literature for negative portrayals of Americans. The most logical explanation is that Wedekind's keen disappointment in not being able to prove the validity of his American citizenship turned him bitter, along with the continuing hardships which he had to suffer, in stark contrast to the wealthy Americans whom he regularly encountered in and around his family.

Two of his brothers had traveled to the United States and had experienced considerable difficulties. It was from his brother Donald that he had heard particularly grim stories, which became the basic material for *Bethel*. Wedekind himself had had an unfortunate love affair with a young American girl, a Miss Isabel Coerne (the teenager appearing in *Der Kammersänger!*), who broke off what Wedekind considered an engagement to marry him.[11] His only recorded encounter with a particularly wealthy American was also associated with a bitter experience, for the Wedekind family estate was sold to an American financier named Jessup.

The growing bitterness toward America, however, is only symptomatic of Wedekind's attitude toward life in general during the years between 1897 and 1905. He shifted the focus of his artistic vision from the universal problems of man and his society to the specific problem of *a* man and his relationship to the world around him. The man was Frank Wedekind, and society was declared guilty as charged of the heinous crime of ridiculing or ignoring the true artist.

But Wedekind did not spare himself in his accusations. Dühring, Nicolo, and Hetmann are also guilty of a serious crime, ironically: they take themselves too seriously, and their inflexibility causes their destruction. Keith almost succumbs at the end, but manages to ward off the temptation. The often exaggerated pathos of the fallen heroes of Wedekind's confessional plays is what saves them from becoming morbid expressions of a self-pitying artist, for one sees Wedekind viewing Wedekind with some misgivings. Yet, there can be little question that these four plays constitute one of the most complete autobiographical statements to be found in all of German literature, a fact certainly obvious to Wedekind himself and to everyone who saw him act in his favorite role, Karl Hetmann. A contemporary described for us what must have been a startling theatrical experience:

This was by far his greatest role, because Hetmann's words, his actions, his frustrations touched at every moment on things from which Wedekind the man suffered the most. Toward the end comes the scene where the director, who is really a circus director, makes the poor wretch an offer which, for the moment, appears to give him one final opportunity. But gradually it becomes clear that Hetmann is wanted as a clown. Before the actor Wedekind staggers off to hang himself, he utters a scream of torment—can anyone who has heard that scream ever forget it?[12]

# CHAPTER 8

## *"The Volcano Appears to Be Extinct"*

THE German satirist Kurt Tucholsky made the above observation
on the occasion of Wedekind's fiftieth birthday in 1914 and
added: "Around the rim stand the respectful tourists and with quiet
fear peer down into the deep hole, believing what they have read in
their Baedeker: Once lava spewed out of here. But that was a long
time ago."[1] Just as suddenly as Wedekind had found his rhythm
and perspective with *Frühlings Erwachen* almost fifteen years
earlier, he lost it after the final revision of *Die Büchse der Pandora*
in 1905. In this relatively brief period of activity, all of his major
works had been written. Tucholsky's evaluation reflects on Wedekind's blurred creative vision during the last decade of his life, when
he produced more than a half-dozen plays which, while re-using the
ideas dealt with in the earlier works, are so narrow in perspective
and so devoid of the generative power typical of his masterpieces
that they appear as mere appendages. Perhaps it was an aftereffect
of the tremendous energy expended in pouring himself into the
personal experience of his autobiographical plays, but never again
did he create a work which possessed the power generated until then.

Or could it have been the shock of acceptance? After Reinhardt's
production of *Frühlings Erwachen* and its unprecedented run of
almost 350 performances in Berlin in 1906, Wedekind assumed the
mantle of elder statesman of the avant-garde. He was no longer the
"enfant terrible," and his marriage to Tilly Newes that year partly
destroyed the myth of Wedekind the Satanist. By 1907 Frank Wedekind was a father, enjoying for himself and his family a measure
of financial stability which, for him, was unheard of. He was revered,
although only by a minority, and recognized even by his enemies as
a writer of some stature. Wedekind's image of himself—as a martyr
changed as he gradually began to accept his new role. All that was

missing was a Faust piece to secure his place in the traditional Pantheon of literary figures; and he obliged the public in 1911, when he wrote *Franziska*. As Paul Fechter notes, "something had come between the creative work and the poet."[2] That Wedekind himself was aware of this seems clear from the fact that he returned to the themes of his earlier works, hoping possibly to rekindle the creative fire. Wedekind's critics have the rare opportunity of studying the works of a writer who, in a sense, is retracing his steps and attempting to apply an earlier formula, which somehow does not quite fit any longer.

## I   Tod und Teufel

The four plays in which Wedekind was exploring his personal relationship to art and society were strikingly uncontroversial. With the exception of Hetmann's new morality, there was very little sexual implication in any of them, and even the critics did not compare the poor deformed reformer to Lulu; he was never treated as an arch-fiend of sorts. The women were, for the most part, conventional, and Alma in *König Nicolo* even suggested a genuine heroine. It was all the more shocking, then, that Wedekind unexpectedly returned to the theme of sexuality in his next play, and in a fashion which produced a jarringly disjointed effect.

*Der Totentanz* originally appeared in 1905, but to avoid confusion with a similarly named play by Strindberg, Wedekind later changed the title to *Tod und Teufel*. It bears some relation to the Lulu plays, and particularly to *Die Büchse der Pandora*, especially since the procurer Casti-Piani is the central figure. He is still a white-slaver and exploiter of prostitutes, but the conception of the character is totally new. He views himself as an apostle of pleasure and takes offense when confronted by the highminded morality of Elfriede von Malchus, a member of the International Association for the Fight Against Procurers (how Wedekind must have hated clubs!).

Elfriede appears at the bordello to save "an unfortunate creature" who has come into Casti-Piani's employ. This German Major Barbara meets her match in moral zeal in Casti-Piani, who passionately suggests to her that she is really hiding her own sensuality by joining such an organization. He urges her to break out of her own emotional confinement. Elfriede steels herself and is about to go to the police when Casti-Piani suddenly grabs her by the throat and forces her to listen to him: "You have wasted so much of your life needlessly trying to save 'Freudenmädchen'! Why not do something to promote *joy* itself for a change!" (V, 13) Within moments Elfriede is completely transformed by the power of Casti-Piani's words. Within minutes of his violent attack on her, she admiringly says: "You are a great man!—You are a noble man!", to which the procurer, somewhat emotionally, replies: "Your words touch on the mortal wound which I brought into the world with me and which some day will cause my death. (*Throws himself into a chair.*) I am—a moralist!" (V, 15–16)

Malchus is somehow overwhelmed by Casti-Piani's newly acquired grandeur and makes a most improbable proposal—of marriage: "Until this hour I have never guessed what the word love meant." But Casti-Piani, stroking the head of the now thoroughly domesticated Elfriede, wants no part of the middle-class family idyl: "As long as I've lived I have loved tigers. With dogs I was always most uncomfortable." (V, 17) He urges Elfriede to forget about marriage and to indulge in the pleasure of the senses without the bothersome ties of traditional morality. In order to convince the erstwhile emancipatress of the genuine righteousness of the "Sinnengenuss," he takes her to a hiding place where they are able to watch Lisika's dealings with a customer of the bordello: "From here we can observe the blissful, serene happiness of two creatures who are exploring sensuality together!" (V, 23)

But Casti-Piani's triumph turns to ashes in his mouth. He overhears Lisika lament the misery of a life which can never satisfy her needs for sensual fulfillment. Casti-Piani listens in horror as she tells the young man of her unhappiness. The gentleman, Herr König, is a sharp Wedekind caricature, a professional writer who plans to publicize the martyrdom of these girls in a forthcoming study, *The Sorrows of Sold Love*. The conversation between Lisika and König, spoken in verse, leaves both Elfriede and Casti-Piani profoundly shaken. Elfriede finally sees her fate clearly before her; to suffer the death of a martyr to her cause, having joyfully discovered that prostitution brings nothing but pain and despair. She begs Casti-Piani to sell her into servitude: "Let me find death in sensuality!" Casti-Piani has looked on with utter disbelief as he hears Lisika tell her customer that sensuality and the life of pleasure is no more than an empty illusion. The procurer, who had actually believed that he was bringing happiness into the world, then hears Elfriede's plea for death and salvation through the sublime *un*happiness of the bordello. This "satanic mockery" is too much for him, and he shoots himself. As the curtain comes down, the mortally wounded moralist-procurer rests in the arms of Elfriede von Malchus, women's emancipator-turned-hopeful-prostitute.

Through the bizarre configurations of character and action, one can still see vestiges of the mythic implications of Eros as a life-force which were encountered in the Lulu plays.[3] But the view is clouded by Wedekind's dragging in of all sorts of Christian allusions, as in the actual motto of the play, taken from Matthew 21:31, which asserts that the publicans and harlots will enter into the kingdom of heaven before the righteous. Elfriede von Malchus also has a biblical namesake, found in John 18:10: "Then Simon Peter, having a sword, drew it and smote the high priest's servant, and cut off his right ear. The servant's name was Malcus." Sokel sees the connection between Elfriede and the biblical Malchus as part of Wedekind's scheme to suggest a distinctly Christian aura, but one reflecting "negative Christianity. Suffering pharisee that her name marks her to be, she considers mutilation to be the essence of holiness."[4] Both she and Casti-Piani pose as Christian moralists of sorts, and each comes to the struggle with the hope of "saving" the other. But Wedekind replaces his normal, honest tendentiousness with a distinctly unchristian nihilism, as if he intended to make a mockery of his theme. The cult of bodily pleasure, which he advocated in theory in the earlier plays, does not find a contented representative in Lisika. There is no cure for her insatiability. No amount of physical love can satisfy her; and to Casti-Piani's utter disillusionment, the life of the prostitute is one of prolonged misery.

For the first time, Wedekind treats the problem of sex in a fashion one might call tasteless, because the author offers no solution, either one way or the other. Casti-Piani's suicide is meaningless, Elfriede's contemplated fate masochistic, and Lisika's cause for unhappiness almost pathological. Wedekind's sincere belief in his proposition, which he presented in everyone of the sexually oriented works from *Die junge Welt* to *Pandora,* turns into a nihilistic alienation from the puppets which he has manipulated. Where there had been meaning, one finds only a void.

II  *"The most modern work I have written"*

In a sense, Wedekind's judgment about his play *Musik* (1906) is quite correct, for in his method there is a great deal that anticipated literary techniques of a much later generation. He found the plot material in the newspaper reports about a sensational story of seduction which took place in Munich, and he searched through as many articles on this event as he could find, preparing a factually accurate documentary. He researched the material and produced a type of dramatic casebook.

The plot seems ready-made for a semi-Naturalistic melodrama. It is the story of Klara Hühnerwadel, a somewhat hysterical music student who has fallen in with Professor Reissner, her tutor, who apparently has been instructing her in other arts, besides music. In the first scene, sinisterly subtitled "Bei Nacht und Nebel," Klara is pregnant and Reissner, to avoid a scandal, sends her to Antwerp to have an abortion, promising her that within a year she will be back singing Wagner with her. But the illegal abortion is discovered by the police, and Klara is placed "hinter schwedischen Gardinen," a euphuism for jail and the title of the second scene. She takes the advice of her jailer to stick to her friends and immediately returns to Reissner, soon to find herself pregnant once again.

Mrs. Reissner, who has patiently observed her husband's love affair, turns for help to a friend the writer Lindekuh, whom Wedekind describes as "a moral monomaniac" who is determined to expose the simple Klara as a scheming, family destroyer. When he becomes convinced of Klara's innocence eventually, he turns all of his fantastic zeal to helping her. In the final episode, for which Wedekind used the same heading he affixes in *König Nicolo* and *Hidalla*, "der Fluch der Lächerlichkeit," Klara stands by the bed of her infant child, who has died during an epidemic. Her fate is much the same as that of the king and Hetmann: "People split with laughter when they hear the story of my misery!" (V, 103) Just then Klara's mother arrives, and mistaking Lindekuh for the villainous Reissner, abuses him while thanking the music teacher "for everything that you've done for my daughter in the past three years."

The key to understanding *Musik* is found in Wedekind's own observations about the play: "The role of Klara is a caricature of a heroine and must not be played with sentimental languish as was done at the first performance in Nürnberg.[5] . . . From Offenbach we have an artistically accomplished form of parodistic music. Why shouldn't there be an artistically worthy parodistic drama also?"[6] The misunderstanding between Wedekind and his public regarding the interpretation of this play is the most reliable measure of its weakness. Wedekind thought he was creating a farce, and the work was accepted as tragedy. At the heart of his parody was, he felt, an attack on outmoded abortion laws and how they affect the rather simple middle class. But, instead, the pitiful Klara, who has managed to let herself be seduced in the most atrociously silly fashion by an equally ineffective voice teacher, becomes the central focus. Klaus Völker's observation best characterizes the deficiency of the play: "On the stage a human being is destroyed, one whose actions can only be described as ridiculous. But it is difficult to laugh."[7] Wedekind fails in *Musik* mainly because he has lost his involvement. Like *Tod und Teufel*, the satire becomes malicious. If its intention was to attack Article 218 of the German Penal Code, which penalized abortion with a prison sentence—as the author said it was—then he obviously was derailed in his main attack. There simply is not sufficient substance in the main characters to justify their role as caricatures. Wedekind's denunciations misfired.

Yet, in his intention and method Wededkind in *Musik* attempted something which, ironically, was to have some significant effect on the theater, in spite of the barrenness of the humor. He permitted his characters to take their plight in great seriousness, while almost instructing the audience to take the opposite point of view. The more Klara bemoans her wretched state, the more hilarious did Wedekind intend her to be. The "message" should come through clearly, he felt, the more detached basically the spectator. Wedekind's didacticism, then, employed the same method that Bertolt Brecht outlined in his notes to the opera *Aufstieg und Fall der Stadt Mahagonny* (*Rise and Fall of the City of Mahagonny*, 1929), and in other writings concerning his concept of Epic Theater. When the actor weeps, the audience should respond with laughter; when tragedy comes and the hero is crushed, the spectator's reaction should be one of disgust at the stupidity of such events.

Wedekind's hinting at an "epic" estrangement of stage and spectator is echoed in the peculiar structure of the play. As Völker recognizes, "*Musik* is not a drama, but rather a chronicle."[8] Wedekind introduces each act as if it were an event in the past tense, attaching an independent motto which anticipates all the forthcoming developments. "Bei Nacht und Nebel" prepares us for Klara's clandestine flight; "Hinter schwedischen Gardinen" anticipates her incarceration; "Vom Regen in die Traufe" ("From the Frying-pan into the Fire") establishes the fact that she will return to Reissner; and "Der Fluch der Lächerlichkeit" ("The Curse of Ridicule") introduces the final emotional outpouring of Klara.

Although Wedekind never gave any specific instructions for the use of these headlines, they seem obviously intended to work as a kind of *Moritat*, which Brecht used so effectively in, for example,

*Die Dreigroschenoper.* With the tension relieved, the audience can sit back and need not worry about the dramatic development, having been informed in advance. The more modern productions of *Musik* take advantage of the technique which has become an integral part of the Brechtian theater, either flashing these signal sentences on an overhead projector before each act, or actually having a street-singer appear on stage to inform the audience personally. Günter Seehaus' comment is worth noting: "Nowhere else in Wedekind's work are so many characteristically Brechtian features anticipated as in *Musik*."[9]

### III  *The Artist Exhibits Himself*

As has already been mentioned, the plays of the last decade of Wedekind's life develop no new thematic material, but return again and again to the successful formulas of the earlier works. In his next two plays, *Die Zensur* (*Censorship,* 1907) and *Oaha* (1908), Wedekind once again uses the stage as a personal pamphlet, but there is a distinct difference between these two autobiographical efforts and the works between *Der Kammersänger* and *Karl Hetmann,* which, in spite of its autobiographical traits, had a universal meaning independent of Wedekind. In *Die Zensur* and *Oaha,* he has pared away all of the peripheral material which relates them to a larger sphere of meaning, so that they must live and die in their intimate relationship with Frank Wedekind himself.

*Die Zensur, eine Theodizee in einem Akt,* is Wedekind's effort to reconcile the evils of censorship with the "righteousness" of his own artistic integrity. Although his reputation had, to a considerable measure, become firmly established by 1907, Wedekind's plays were still fair game to governmental censors, who seemed to take particular pleasure in banning them, regardless of their content. The author makes no effort to hide the fact that Frank Wedekind's plays are the central issue of *Die Zensur.* The conflict is exposed in a dialogue between the writer Buridan and the private secretary of the Emperor, Dr. Cajetan Prantl, who has come, on Buridan's request, to discuss the censoring of the writer's tragedy *Pandora,* which also happened to be Wedekind's most controversial play. At the time of the writing of *Die Zensur,* litigation was still pending in the high courts of Germany, which ultimately permitted *Pandora* to be performed. Publishers often published excerpts from the *Pandora* trial in editions of the play.[10] Obviously, it was this sensational series of events which prompted Wedekind to put his case before the public.

Prantl presents the state's case when he accuses Buridan of cynical nihilism (a charge repeatedly made by Wedekind's critics) and asserts that the writer's reputation as a blasphemer is justified by his literary output. Buridan defends himself much as Wedekind had in the foreword to a recent edition of *Pandora*, which became a regular addendum to subsequent editions:

Can you show me anything at all in my works which in the end did not have as its intention the consideration and honoring of a code of conformity, which we all pay homage to? In none of my works have I set down the good as evil, or the evil as good. I have never falsified events which grow out of the actions of human beings. (V, 125)

Prantl is astonished to discover that Buridan is so serious about his art, having heard that he was no more than an anti-social Bohemian interested only in outraging his audiences. Buridan takes advantage of Prantl's sympathy to profess his belief in God as well as in the society and social order which the Almighty has constructed. His only purpose, he insists, has been to educate, improve, and instruct his fellow man. Point by point, Buridan admirably defends himself against the accusations of his adversary. At the point where he expounds on his theory of physical beauty as an enlightened concept, which is in no way conflicting with morality, Buridan's provocative mistress Kadidja enters, dressed enticingly in a new costume. Prantl points an accusing finger at this apparition: "There she is! The enemy! The temptress! The snake of Paradise!" (V, 133) Prantl leaves, now more than ever convinced of Buridan's evil influence.

The second dialogue between the victorious Kadidja and Buridan, who is distraught at having been interrupted just when it appeared that he was convincing Prantl of his sincerity now commences. When she mocks the censor's puritanism, Buridan admits that he has been shaken by Prantl. He must free himself from Kadidja for a while, in order to find himself and, hopefully, a "cure" for his malady, which is the attachment to Kadidja: "I must have ugliness before me for a time, nothing but ugliness." (V, 139)

Kadidja, who owes everything to Buridan's instruction and education in the art of physical pride, sees his pangs of conscience as her death sentence. Her artist will throw her off, in order to secure a place in society. She jumps onto a balcony and prepares to leap. Suddenly Buridan comes to his senses and admits that, for a moment, he had felt the urge to discard her: "For only a moment I had forgotten who you are." But Kadidja, like Lulu, has a vision of her numbered days. She sees her only protector deserting her. As Buridan pleads with her to come down from the ledge, Kadidja leaps to her death, leaving the writer distractedly crying to himself: "Oh God, how incomprehensible you are. . . ." (V, 140)

*Die Zensur* is inescapably one of the most personal plays ever written for the stage, and for that reason it has serious limitations. It seems that Wedekind, in the guise of Buridan, is questioning the whole purpose of his artistic life. Buridan is confronted with a tremendously difficult decision: which world to choose? In the Prantl-Kadidja conflict Buridan is torn between his desire for acceptance and his need for artistic freedom. There was no hesitation on Wedekind's part in identifying completely with Buridan; he said that he should have titled the play *Exhibitionism* or *Personal Statement*.[11] And in the momentary rejection of Kadidja one sees the outcast renegade Frank Wedekind's desperate effort at gaining entrance to the world of respectability. Kadidja, aware that this is not perhaps just a temporary, or even insincere gesture on the part of the shrewd artist, accepts her rejection and envisions her ultimate fate. There is no other recourse but suicide.

Unlike Thomas Mann's great confessional story *Tonio Kröger* (1903), which also deals with the problem of the artist in search of his world, Wedekind could not inject a sense of detachment from himself. Everywhere, even in the manuscript, Wedekind makes it perfectly clear that he is discussing himself.[12] Drama here became a type of therapy on a highly personal level. *Die Zensur* does not reach out toward the audience with a universal meaning, but rather extends inward to its own creator.

## IV  Oaha, Die Satire der Satire

*Oaha* is still another play for the "insider," perhaps even more so than *Die Zensur*. Even the dedication excites the Wedekind enthusiast, for the writer honors his wife, almost as a token of reconciliation after causing her considerable consternation in the writing of *Die Zensur*. It was obviously unavoidable that Tilly should see herself as the real-life Kadidja, and therefore as the force which kept her husband from gaining respectability. By analogy, she became identified with everything that Kadidja represented. (Tilly did not remain peeved long enough to deny herself the role of Kadidja in the premiere performance which took place in 1909, with the Wedekinds playing the leading roles.) *Oaha*, following directly on the heels of an autobiographical play, is the clearest indication of the difficulty Wedekind encountered in developing new ideas. Once again he turned to what almost amounts to a documentation of his personal life, this time the love-hate relationship with his publisher Albert Langen, one of Wedekind's first supporters and the founder of *Simplizissimus*, with whom Wedekind had had a serious falling out during the writer's imprisonment. The main conflict of this "satire of satire" is between Georg Sterner, publisher of a satirical journal called *Till Eulenspiegel*, and his staff. Wedekind made no effort whatsoever to mask what to the entire literary world of Munich were known facts and faces. Sterner is no doubt Langen. He is forced to flee to Paris because of an inflammatory poem attacking the Kaiser which appeared in his journal. His relationship to his underlings graphically emerges in the first exchange with the writer Max Bouterweck, a "gekränkte Leberwurst" and intended to be Wedekind, the injured party:

Sterner: What do you wish?
Bouterweck: Money.
Sterner: For what?
Bouterweck: So that I can get something to eat for lunch. So that I can buy a pair of shoes which I've needed for two weeks. (V, 147)

The literary detective should not have too much difficulty in identifying several other luminaries who appear in the play. Langen's father-in-law, the noted Scandinavian writer Björnstjerne Björnson, is represented as Ole Olestierna, "poet and politician (tall and self-conscious)." The head of *Till Eulenspiegel*'s art department is Kuno Konrad Laube, whose alliterative name points directly to the famous *Simplizissimus* illustrator Thomas Theodor Heine. Wedekind exchanged the names of two German writers who were identified with the "Jung Deutschland" movement: both Heine and Laube spent time together in exile in Paris. The peculiar dress of the writer Dr. Kilian betrays his real-life model, Ludwig Thoma, the Bavarian humorist—a fact which did not escape Thoma and which led to some friction between the two men.[13] Besides these luminaries, Wedekind satirized several lesser known personalities in his Munich circle, but the greatest blast was reserved for Langen.

It was to his circus experience that Wedekind returned in order to show the relationship between Sterner and his employees. In *Die Zensur,* the relationship between Buridan and Kadidja was clearly one of "Tierbändiger and Tier," in the Schwigerling-Katharina sense. Buridan was the trainer using the riding whip first, then discarding it after his pupil had learned her lessons:

Kadidja: You instructed me in the art of the riding whip.
Buridan: The servant needs a riding whip to beat rugs, it is of no more
  use to me. (V, 112)

In *Oaha,* the struggle between Sterner and his associates is once again presented in terms of the relationship between trainer and menagerie; but Sterner is not interested in elevating the state of his subjects, so that they might some day attain freedom from bondage. He constantly repeats the phrase "im Zaum halten," to keep in rein; and Dr. Kilian speaks for the rest of the group when he describes himself and his colleagues as "a strayed herd of cattle" under Sterner's control. Indeed, they refer to one another as cattle or, more often, dogs. Sterner is no match for them, for they are the feckless idealists, while he is a composite of Keith-Launhart, a brutal and brilliant exploiter perpetually one step ahead of everyone.

In fact, Wedekind makes some obvious references to Keith, especially as Sterner is about to flee to Paris. For a moment he contemplates taking a revolver along with him, in case desperate measures are called for; but he gingerly throws the pistol down, preferring to reject any such black thoughts of suicide out of hand. He is the complete villain, interested only in profit. When the notorious poem appears, Sterner actually hopes for confiscation, knowing what this publicity would do for sales. When he is faced with police action, he displays a monumental cowardice and makes every effort to place all the blame on the poet Bouterweck.

But his most flagrant breach of ethics is artistic, when he hires a deaf-and-dumb Swiss idiot named Oaha who, Sterner hopes, will inspire the magazine to greater heights of wit and humor. Wedekind's attack here is directed as much against the public's level of intelligence as it is against Langen. Oaha (his name is another example of Wedekind's American fetish) represents the public's idea of wit and humor. His function is to write captions for cartoons. He sits mutely in Sterner's office, reviewing pictures. When he suddenly explodes into laughter at the sight of a particular frame, he writes his reaction on a blackboard, and his remarks become the text for the picture. This idiot's delight is in perfect harmony with the world's funny bone.

The satire is often too cryptic to have universal meaning, but in one instance Wedekind did create a delightful character in the figure of still another American, one Wanda Washington, who in the dramatis personae is already described as "durch und durch unecht." What he actually makes of Wanda is a delightful parody of his most famous female creation, Lulu. She is a madcap who is desperately in love with Sterner and throws herself at him at every occasion:

Wanda (*Bursts through the opened door of Sterner's private room in his office, throws her arms around his neck, and kisses him passionately*): What a moment! George! George! I've never been adored by anyone like this before! What a sweet, evil, stupid wretch you are!
Sterner (*Somewhat taken back*): How did you get into my private room?
Wanda: I've been sitting there since nine o'clock this morning. All I know is that I've had a terrible yearning for you! Last night I couldn't sleep. . . (*passionately*) I bear no guilt for my superhuman desire for you! (V, 221–23)

In a blatant imitation of Lulu's end as a prostitute supporting her lover, Wanda makes a supreme effort to gain admittance to a bordello, but is caught up in a bureaucratic entanglement: "Two years ago I was all set in a house of joy in Venice. But somehow they found out that my papers weren't in order. Oh, how I envy those simple country girls, whose papers are always so meticulously in order!" (V, 224)

As a private parody intended for an audience intimately acquainted with the objects of Wedekind's satire, *Oaha* belongs to the sub-genre of literary parodies which German authors such as Grabbe and Heinrich Heine occasionally indulged in. For the literary historian, *Oaha* is an interesting period piece. But beyond that Wedekind gave no life to the caricatures, and Kutscher, Wedekind's intimate friend and apologist, admitted that it was his weakest play, because of the very nature of its subject matter.

The objects of Wedekind's satire, however, immediately became interested parties when the play was published in 1908, and there was much talk among the staff of *Simplizissimus* about paying Wedekind back in kind. It was Ludwig Thoma, the most qualified wit among them, who picked up his pen; and his reply appeared in the October 26 issue of that year, in the form of a dialogue written by one Peter Schlemihl and entitled *Der Satanist,* a name often attached to Wedekind by some of his more theologically oriented adversaries.

The action of the playlet takes place before a court of justice in Leipzig (the scene of Wedekind's trial of *Majestätsbeleidigung*), where the accused, Franz Wedelgrind, a "satanic" poet, has been called to account for an insulting poem about the nation's ruler. Wedelgrind is a frightened wretch, begs for mercy and claims that he has always been a royalist. Out of necessity he has been forced to hide his true allegiance to the crown, fearing that his publisher would fire him if the truth were to be known. His hunger drove him to his present precarious situation, and if the court would show mercy, he promises to begin a new life, give up all thoughts of insulting the monarch, and become a model citizen. Furthermore, to show his good intentions, he gives an outline of a project which is to mark the turning point in his life. Wedelgrind intends to dramatize the most intimate feelings of a very close friend—an obvious reference to Wedekind's constant dramatic self-analysis. From now on, he promises the court, he will be a reform-minded writer: "I shall bury the past, everything that I stood for, and every-one who stood near me. I shall be a good boy! I shall be loyal!" The judge eyes him ironically and notes that the repentant gentle-man before him still seems quite satanic, whereupon Wedelgrind shrugs his shoulders and offers, as his final defense, a recasting of the last line from *Der Marquis von Keith*: "Poetry is a roller-coaster. . . ."

Thoma and his circle felt that Wedekind's parody in *Oaha* went too far even as a satire. The image which emerged of Bouterweck as a healthy, idealistic artist surrounded by eccentric pseudo-intellec-tuals did more than outrage plausibility. Many felt that Wedekind's role as the uncrowned king of the anti-establishment was not at all justified, that at heart Wedekind was a bourgeois manqué, who would abandon his beliefs at the slightest sign of pressure from the opposition. In the light of what Wedekind suffered during the dying years of the nineteenth century for remaining faithful to his muse, this would seem an unfair criticism. Also, it was during the first decade of the twentieth century, while Wedekind's reputation grew, that he became a fairly active social pamphleteer; and he enjoyed the hatred of the conservative press as much for his position on militarism, politicians, the death sentence, and social welfare as for his plays.

The greatest irony, however, appeared in 1914 when Wedekind shocked many of his friends by giving full support to Germany's involvement in World War I. Their anger must have been considerable, and doubly so, because Wedekind's advocacy of his nation's cause had little effect on his reputation. Those who were prepared to idolize him did so regardless of inconsistencies or criticism. They still remembered the role he had played only a few years earlier as a symbol for all the suppressed writers of Germany, and they were not about to abandon him.

## V  Schloss Wetterstein

Considering that Wedekind had not produced an "original" work in five years, and had done no more than rehash already used thematic material, it is not surprising that in 1910 he should have returned to the idea which motivated the Lulu plays, which, at that time were causing a considerable sensation all over Europe.[14] But conceivably Wedekind took up this highly controversial theme once again to reassure his followers and colleagues that he was still "das Schreckbild der Moralisten," the terror of the moralists. Moreover, the resulting play, *Schloss Wetterstein*, is such an incredible distortion of Wedekind's original concept of sex and society that it offended both critics and admirers. If there ever was a play by Wedekind which should have been banned (as *Schloss Wetterstein* was immediately), it was this one; not so much for its offensiveness, as for the revelation that it makes of Wedekind's inability to deal meaningfully with his ideas. Sokel suggests that Wedekind had a "rebellious wish for martyrdom," that he enjoyed being the figure of hate of an outraged community.[15] If so, *Schloss Wetterstein*'s provocative exhibitionism accomplished that end.

Essentially it is a family drama with emphasis on the perversity of the Wettersteins. Rüdiger von Wetterstein is a debauched, Gothic villain who, for five years, has been trying to win the affections of Leonore Gystrow, finally killing her husband in a duel arranged with great precision. Once again we find Wedekind parodying, this time *Richard III*. Like Shakespeare's hunchbacked manipulator, Rüdiger courts the young widow, baldly confessing that he has rigged the duel, and that he has made all of these elaborate plans only for this very moment. Leonore is shocked, then gradually won over by the very effrontery of Rüdiger's deed. She consents to marry him, and they establish a household with Leonore's daughter, Effie.

In the second act, Rüdiger finds himself in the hands of a financial cutthroat, Meinhard Luckner, who is perfectly willing to liquidate Rüdiger's debts if he is given Leonore in exchange. Luckner is attracted to her because of her great hate for him. He wants no part of marital love and affection, only the physical pleasures of Leonore. Rüdiger encourages his wife to respond to Luckner's proposition, but she refuses. However, Effie understands her mother's newest suitor and urges her to profess genuine love for him. Leonore's absence gives Rüdiger the opportunity to make some incestuous advances to Effie, who is all too eager to play the game. At the height of this "family discussion," they hear a shot and discover that Luckner, out of disgust with Leonore's protestations of love, has killed himself.

Because of Rüdiger's operations, the family is financially ruined and left only with a castle which Rüdiger has inherited. Here, in grand Victorian splendor, Effie realizes her aim in life. Under the direction of an impresario named Karl Salzmann, she has established herself in a magnificent bordello. She is free and independent, having married a middle-class businessman, stripped him of his wealth, and left him to commit suicide. She supports her mother and step-father in their old age, and life in the castle seems very comfortable. Great excitement prevails as they await the arrival of a mysterious American millionaire, Mr. Chagnaral Tschamper. His reputation as a Bluebeard has already reached the castle. Several girls have unaccountably died in his presence, although he has established his innocence in every instance. For his part, Mr. Tschamper's request seems morbid and somewhat mad. He will pay $100,000 for the privilege of dying in front of a naked woman! To Effie this seems only reasonable, and she is prepared to honor the contract she makes with Tschamper. What she does not know is that he has refined the techniques of Jack the Ripper, although he is just as effective. The sensation-seeking millionaire gets his thrills from observing the death pangs of others. When Effie and Tschamper are alone in the room, he is apparently prepared to drink the glass of poison which he has set before himself. Before he drinks, he asks her to relate the saddest event of her life. Effie hesitates, not wanting to create a mood of sadness. But she is drawn out by Tschamper's pleading and relates the events which caused her the greatest pain. Their mutual pain—hers real, his feigned—mingles together, until Effie feels a genuine affinity for Tschamper. When he pretends to drink from the poisoned glass, she cries out:

No! You must live!
Because I love you! Did ever man and woman
Find one another better matched
Than you and I? For the first time, existence
No longer grins at me with hollow eyes.[16]

She sees him as a fellow sufferer, a spiritual kin:

You need a woman who gives all to you.
I lack a man to whom to give myself. (VI, 97)

Tschamper asks Effie if she really believes in sacrificing herself for him. As proof of her loyalty, she begs him to allow her to drink the poison. Tschamper continues to play with her emotions, exciting her to the point where she grabs the glass and drinks the contents. Tschamper sits back in his easy chair enjoying what Fechter describes as "the bliss of watching someone die." Effie's death struggle is violent, and he is not disappointed:

Ah, how beautiful! Ah, what wonder!
Thank you, my child. None other was so sweet.
(VI, 98)

Wedekind wrote the entire act in blank verse, thinking that here was the material for elevated language. Instead, we are given a display of sadism and hard-core voyeurism almost unparalleled in serious dramatic literature. Effie, the ultimate reincarnation of Lulu, suffers because, unlike Lulu, she is a real person whose sexual excessiveness throughout the play is completely devoid of any mythic implication; so what we are left with is nothing more than a nymphomaniac. Wedekind does not develop a consistent moral point of view, and her perversity is never pardonable, never tied to an expression of belief.

Luckner is still another version of the brutal American-style capitalist, the German counterpart of which is the Sterner-Launhart type of predator-swindler. To make certain that the image of the American robber-baron comes across to his audience, Wedekind sprinkles some bizarre figures of speech into his lines, such as when Luckner threatens Rüdiger with financial ruin:

Luckner: Sie wollten der fünfte Mensch des Erdballs sein: Rockefeller, Morgan, Krupp, Carnegie und Wetterstein!

Rüdiger: Es ist mir unmöglich, über irgendeinen Gedanken nachzuden-
  ken. Lassen Sie mir bis morgen Zeit.
Luckner: Nicht um Chicago! (VI, 38)

Once again, it is clear that what was admirable in Keith is debased
in Luckner. Through the years, as Wedekind confronted the capi-
talistic system, he grew more and more contemptible of it, even
losing Keith's delight in exploiting it. Keith had taken great pleasure
in being mistaken for an American railroad king. In *Schloss Wetterstein*, America is represented by two industrialists who are perverse
to the extreme.

With its suicides, murders, and erotic sensationalism, *Schloss
Wetterstein* is more like an Elizabethan grotesque than anything
else Wedekind wrote. What remains a puzzle is why he would suddenly turn to such an obviously controversial treatment which has
such little artistic merit while being prurient beyond any necessity
to express purpose or idea. One inevitably falls back on an inade-
quate and amateurish analysis of Wedekind himself. Either for
financial reasons or motivated by his own image of himself as a
suddenly respected writer he felt compelled to write such a play.
The financial gain would have come most likely in the form of
controversy, which would give his other works additional exposure
in the theaters. But given the nature of his self-image, the second
reason seems more plausible. His last few plays did not receive the
critical attention he had hoped for. Even the censor had demonstrated that with few isolated exceptions, they were fit for public
presentation. As he approached his fiftieth birthday, possibly sensing
a lull in interest, he produced a literary potboiler that unquestionably
contained all the Wedekind ingredients, except the artistic sensibility. If his intention was to create a storm of controversy, he
certainly succeeded. Knowing the mentality of the official censors,
Wedekind had to realize that the play would be banned. When it
was staged in 1919 after Wedekind's death, even Kutscher made
an observation which is astonishing considering his attitude toward
Wedekind: "The banning of the play was justified, for it simply
could not have a proper effect on a large group of people. It is best
suited for a literary audience."[17]

## VI  *"Franziska, dieser weibliche Faust"*—Paul Fechter

It was time, in 1911, for Wedekind to acknowledge his relationship
to Goethe and to deal with the Faust story. Even he could not ignore

the barbed criticisms which hinted that Wedekind was intellectually bankrupt and could no longer create new ideas for the stage. For this very reason, *Franziska* is one of the most successful of his late plays, for Wedekind forced himself away from the themes he had been dealing with over the years; and the new material breathed a freshness into an airy mixture of prose and verse which forms the body of this "modern mysterium." From Goethe Wedekind took the free theatrical inventiveness of *Faust;* and for the first time since *Frühlings Erwachen* he moved out of a fourth-wall conventional set into the free air.

Yet there is much vintage Wedekind. Who else but Wedekind would have created a female Faust? Franziska is a restless, attractive young woman who is bored with living with her mother. She wants no part of marriage, having observed the unhappy state of life of her parents. She desires pleasure, but does not know where to find it. The answer comes with a knock at her window by Veit Kunz, an insurance agent from Berlin, who comes to her with a proposition. In exchange for two years of freedom from care and a thorough indoctrination into the pleasures of life, Franziska must promise to become Kunz's devoted wife. Franziska, sick of the dull and unappetizing life around her, readily agrees, even to the condition that she must disguise herself as a man.

Wedekind stays remarkably close to the action in Goethe's play, and the parallels are obvious throughout. There is an "Auerbachs Keller" scene which takes place in a wild nightclub called "Clara's Place," but the public in attendance is strictly Wedekind, with perhaps a bow to Schnitzler's *Der grüne Kakadu* (1898). The nobility casually mixes with prostitutes, elegant writers sit with down-and-out workers. For the first time in years, Wedekind's language takes on the hypnotic quality which is so typical of the earlier plays. Lofty artistic insights alternate with obscenities and a seemingly uncontrolled stream-of-consciousness. The hackneyed and the esoteric blend in this most interesting scene; and for a moment, Wedekind is at his very best.

Wedekind's "Gretchen Episode" is, on the other hand, quite far-fetched; in its improbability it is more reminiscent of his ballets. Franziska, now called Franz, is enjoying considerable fame as a singer and is "married" to a young lady, Sophie, who somehow has not discovered Franziska's true identity. Franziska, to her dismay, discovers that she is pregnant, and Kunz is the father-to-be. Wedekind introduces the counterpart to Gretchen's brother Valentine in

[ 114 ]

the figure of Sophie's brother, Oberstleutnant Dirckens, who discovers Franziska's disguise. He wants to revenge his sister's lost honor. But for Sophie the shock and scandal is too much, and she shoots herself.

Soon Wedekind abandons the rational world of *Faust I* for the symbolic realm of *Faust II*, and Veit Kunz and Franziska experience a variety of bizarre episodes, until finally the two years have passed. Kunz is satisfied that Franziska is purged of her desire for excitement and, relinquishing his role as Mephistopheles, he marries her and settles down to a life of everyday contentment. The subsequent development is unexpected, except for those who realize that it was almost impossible for Wedekind to keep himself out of his plays. Kunz now starts a new career as a writer of "mysteries," in which his newly acquired wife acts. Gradually, the character of Veit Kunz merges with that of Wedekind himself; and what is revealed next, if it is autobiographical and factual, must have caused some raised eyebrows from the public which understood Wedekind's necessity for dramatizing himself on stage.

Kunz collapses when he discovers that Franziska has had an affair with the actor Breitenbach. The center of the dramatic tension shifts to Veit Kunz. Wedekind's Mephisto, who had fallen into the temptation of accepting a state of contented marital bliss, realizes that he has been defrauded by his own desires to believe in something—in this case, the traditional institution of marriage. With a final grandiose gesture of rejection, he attempts to take his own life, but even in this he fails. He is not even permitted to enjoy the tranquillity of death. Veit Kunz lives on to suffer the repeated humiliation in his knowledge that he has a great necessity and inner urge for the commonplace, in spite of his Mephistophelean "Geist, der stets verneint."

In motherhood Franziska finds contentment and a purpose in life. She lives with the painter Karl Almer and her son Vietralf (named after her two former lovers). When Kunz and Breitenbach visit her in her lovely country retreat, they find a Franziska they do not know. She has come to understand the limitations of the world and has learned to make peace with them, not to struggle against forces she cannot alter.

It is almost inconceivable that Wedekind should have written a play in justification of conventional marriage and motherhood, two institutions which he battled for most of his adult life. But when we consider the extent to which his personal experiences find their

way into his literary works, it makes somewhat more sense. Wedekind, after all, was, by this time, the father of two children, and,
as has already been mentioned, he accepted this new responsibility
in great earnestness. Almer's remarks in the last scene herald a new
voice of optimism for Wedekind: "You see, the world is really not
as bad as some die-hard pessimists would make us believe." (VI,
216) Fechter, on the other hand, would have us view this pleasant
state of affairs as "the bitterest derision which Wedekind ever made
of the developmental possibilities of woman—and of his own proph-
ecies."[18] In an effort to make Wedekind's position on the question of
women consistent throughout his works, Fechter has stretched the
point, because the paradoxical irony which would convert Franziska's contentment to satire is missing. Wedekind does not suggest
an act of revenge by ending Franziska's Faustian quest in a trivial
existence. Her acceptance of motherhood and marriage, and stability
in general, are genuine.

Wedekind's "Freudenmädchen" has run the full cycle. She has
come home to roost, after a tempestuous history of freedom from
society, a confrontation which resulted in society's destruction, and
finally society's revenge. What had been an instinctive, primal urge
for gratification of the life-instinct settles down to a placid acceptance of the social responsibilities within the framework of a civilized,
mature culture. Lulu has finally been domesticated. Franziska's
renunciation of dissatisfaction represents the taming of "das wilde,
schöne Tier," which was her essential nature at the beginning of her
search for happiness. Wedekind has abandoned Eros in favor of
civilization.

## VII

*"The intellectual and poetic reputation of Frank Wedekind is
justly so great, that one naturally gives credit where credit is
often not due."—Alfred Polgar*

Like Gerhart Hauptmann in the twilight of his career, Wedekind,
in the final years of his life turned to classical myth and verse drama,
as if to give additional weight to their reputation. The year that
produced *Simson* also saw the publication of the *Wedekindbuch*
and the adulation of almost every literary luminary in Germany.
With few exceptions, Wedekind faithfully adhered to the biblical
material, and the result is a wooden, at times pompous, play. In

one episode, however, he could not resist the temptation to justify to himself once again, and for this purpose he re-created his own situation. The blinded Samson is transformed into a court singer, lamenting his own fate. His greatest pain is his humiliation, an artist mocked and ridiculed by a vulgar audience jealous of his strength and sensitivity. One might have expected more from Wedekind in dealing with one of the Bible's great male-female struggles, but after the reconciliation with life in *Franziska,* he was simply no longer prepared to engage in the battle.

The most interesting aspect of the play actually is the disproportionate amount of critical acclaim it received. Kutscher sponsored a reading in his theater seminar at the university in Munich before a packed classroom, and the premiere performance at the Lessingtheater in Berlin met with weighty approval. The *Vossische Zeitung* called *Simson* "the most significant theatrical event of the year," a sentiment echoed in numerous prestigious periodicals and newspapers.[19]

Irony never seemed to be far from Wedekind. This, one of his least objectionable plays based on material found in Scripture, was banned nonetheless by the Munich censor. For Wedekind, this act of censorship was incomprehensible and the last straw. In part, it could have been responsible for his turning his back on the political position which he had held, and about which he had been quite outspoken during the past decade. Wedekind had been a vocal opponent of the military castes and the type of cloak-and-dagger diplomacy which had marked European power politics since the formation of a unified Germany.

But he was also a realist, and his statement "one must run with the pack" illustrates a firm belief in the doctrine of enlightened self-interest found later in Bert Brecht's actions under the Ulbricht regime in East Germany, part of which has become the material for Günter Grass's play *Die Plebeer proben den Aufstand,* in which Grass accuses Brecht of betraying his principles in order to secure favor in the eyes of the East German government during the workers' revolt of 1953. Ludwig Thoma and others hinted that Wedekind had leaned toward the same position in writing *Oaha;* and their suspicions were born out in Wedekind's *Bismarck.* Written in 1915, it is in every sense a propaganda piece, glorifying the Iron Chancellor's role in creating a unified Germany. Wedekind was pedantically objective in retelling the story of Bismarck's rise to power. His main sources were the letters and memoirs of the chancellor, and he was remarkably faithful to them in creating his dialogue. Anecdotes, jokes, and epigrams which were credited to Bismarck find their way into the play, which, in five acts, chronicles the years between 1863 and 1866, centering on the defeat of Austria and the growth of Prussia under Bismarck. It is a dramatization of a segment of European history, and unlike in *Simson*, Wedekind stuck doggedly to the facts. He avoids any hint of female involvement, and the three women who appear have very little dramatic function. Bismarck dominates the action completely, and his political acumen, along with the vision of a future Germany, set the jingoist tone of the work.

The apologists are numerous and all agree that it was out of expediency that Wedekind made such an incredible about-face from political liberal to wholehearted supporter of the empire. Both his friend Kutscher and his editor Friedenthal point to the number of German intellectuals who were caught up in the nationalistic hysteria of the war.[20] But for Wedekind, there was an additional motivation which for him transcended all political and idealistic reasons to reverse his stand. At the very outset of hostilities, Wedekind's plays were completely removed from the German repertory. His works disappeared, on the grounds that they would undermine the morale of the people on the homefront. In spite of the public pronouncements which he had made as early as 1914 supporting the German war machine, it did not remove the stigma of immorality. If he was to keep himself before the German public, he had to create a work which would be acceptable by the standards of the day. The result was *Bismarck*. The censor gave immediate approval.

Yet *Bismarck* did not have its premiere until 1926, in of all places, Weimar, the capital of the first German Republic. Wedekind, who had written a work so atypical for him, only in the hope of getting his name before the public once again, had miscalculated. Max Reinhardt was eager to produce the play in the *Deutsches Theater* in Berlin. Rehearsals had already been scheduled when word came down from highly placed government officials: the play was not to be performed, on the grounds that it would have been in bad taste to dramatize an earlier conflict between Germany and Austria, at a time when they were allies fighting a common cause.

## VIII   *The Final Curtain*

There are several touches in Wedekind's last play, *Herakles*, written in 1917—the year before his death—which indicate that this was to be his swan-song. The problem of this "bastard between God and man" is that of the outsider searching for a means of existence in a world which is fundamentally alien to him. Wedekind's Herakles is the most miserable of creatures, half-human and half-god, burning with a divine ardor which goes beyond any earthly compassion to understand his plight. Only in death can he hope to find peace. It is this personal insinuation that Wedekind makes in Herakles that gives the play its meaning for us. Like Simson, Herakles has been both blessed by the gods with superhuman strength and cursed by them, so that contentment in the world of humans is impossible. Herakles has one burning desire: "Mensch zu sein." He spends his entire life in a search for the meaning of human existence. Only in the flaming death which Dejaneira unwittingly causes does Herakles finally find a sort of contentment, a peace of mind devoid of the strife and agony which had marked his life.

In the mind of the perhaps overenthusiastic student of Wedekind, Herakles takes on the image of Shakespeare's Prospero in *The Tempest,* a conscious creation on the part of an author to indicate a swan-song. Although Wedekind left behind a large amount of material, he was not working on another manuscript the year he died, and we are left with *Herakles* as the final document of a tremendously self-conscious author who saw himself inevitably reflected in his primary characters. It is this identity which most likely saves *Herakles,* for in his final effort at verse tragedy, Wedekind was no more successful than he had been in the past. The stentorian tones are hollow, and the language of poetry does not come alive often enough to save the play. But the touching and ominous forewarning of the approaching death of the author gives the work a weight and sense of mystery which is communicated to Wedekind's audience, ever eager to have this most self-conscious of writers reveal his most personal feelings even to the moment of his death.

# CHAPTER 9

# *Wedekind's Prose*

I T is only natural that a study of this sort should concentrate on that phase of Wedekind's creativity which has given him his fame, namely his plays. Yet his other literary creations deserve at least a brief analysis. As a lyric poet, Wedekind demonstrated that he had little sympathy with the traditional meaning of the word "lyric." His poems reflect a brutality and a clinical cynicism which often go beyond the scope of what his plays reflected. In spite of this dark vision, Wedekind considered himself a folk-singer, because his material had popular roots. The poet found his particular muse in the back streets of Munich. He was one of the first German lyricists to find inspiration in city life, in the sordid realities of death, murder, and prostitution. With his guitar in hand, Wedekind sang, like a twentieth-century minstrel, of the wretchedness of his time.

Wedekind's poetry does not need "rediscovery," having inspired a whole generation of poets, beginning with Brecht whose own genius transcended the lyrical artistry of Wedekind while securing his place as a major influence. But in the case of the considerable body of Wedekind's narrative prose, there is no such influence, and as a result, the perhaps overzealous Wedekind scholar is tempted to "rediscover," to search for a significance where others have found none. For Wedekind's prose writings have elicited hardly any critical attention. These dozen short stories are rarely anthologized; and unlike his impact as a dramatist and lyricist, Wedekind's force as a writer of prose fiction has made no appreciable contribution to German or European letters.[1] This fact is all the more astonishing, for even the most cautious critic would have to admit that a few stories merit considerable attention, and one rivals almost any short story in the German language.

Wedekind's short stories and his one novel, *Mine-Haha, oder Über die körperliche Erziehung der jungen Mädchen* (Concerning the Physical Education of Young Girls), were, for the most part, completed before 1900. The first collection of prose appeared in 1897, along with much of the early poetry and three of the pantomimes, in a volume entitled *Die Fürstin Russalka* (Princess Russalka). The short stories were published once again in 1905 (with minor additions) under the title *Feuerwerk* (Fireworks). *Mine-Haha* was brought out by the Insel-Verlag in 1901. A variety of short pieces, some never before published, appeared in the *Nachlass* volumes of the definitive edition of Kutscher and Joachim Friedenthal, which Langen-Müller published in 1924.

Each of the pieces bears a striking resemblance to at least one of Wedekind's dramatic works. *Die Fürstin Russalka* is a companion piece to *Die junge Welt* and *Frühlings Erwachen*. The central figure, Frau Dr. Rappart (she appears also in *Die junge Welt*), is telling a female companion of her spiritual development. She narrates her own story. As a teenager she had been incredibly naïve, believing that all children came from God and solely with His permission, since all parents are first united in the sanctity of the church. Like Wendla Bergmann in *Frühlings Erwachen*, she had been utterly unaware of the biological basis of sex. Her more enlightened sister attempts to educate her, but the young girl, at that time still the Princess Russalka, refuses to believe the clinical account her sister had given her. In order to refute her sister's theory, she offers herself to the Duke of Galliera, a visiting nobleman. Russalka's strong Catholicism and good luck seems to bear out her beliefs, for her relationship with the Duke produces no children. Some years later, however, after having married Galliera and still having produced no children, Russalka begins to fear that she was barren. Her husband proves to be unfaithful and fathers a child of Russalka's cousin. Russalka, now a matured and embittered young woman, abandons her religion in favor of atheism and leaves her native Berlin. She becomes a "modern" woman, cuts her hair mannishly short, wears men's clothing, and supports the women's emancipation movement. At the premiere of Ibsen's *Hedda Gabler*, she meets Dr. Rappart, a Social Democratic leader. He urges her to abandon this unnatural masculinity and marry him. But Russalka is still insecure and frightened of her inability to have children. She attempts suicide, is saved by Rappart, whom she marries and soon thereafter bears a child.

This brings Frau Dr. Rappart's narrative up-to-date. She has found contentment, she tells her friend Baroness Hohenwart, who feels inspired by the former noblewoman's story, but has one nagging regret: was it necessary for her to give up her nobility?

The negative attitude of Wedekind's heroine keeps this story from attaining a meaningful purpose. Russalka is a failure as an adolescent and wife, looks foolish as a feminist, and ends up as a smugly contented bourgeois. Yet Wedekind's irony does not quite carry off the attempted satire. There is little mastery of narrative tension, or even characterization. In his dramas, Wedekind could successfully cope with marionettes whose personalities had little basis in reality. But this becomes a narrative weakness, especially since Russalka dominates the "stage" of this brief tale. The reader hopes in vain to be convinced by some part of her personality.

Like almost all of Wedekind's prose narratives, *Russalka* is couched in the form of the classical German "flashback novella." This particular device is quite fitting for this story, since it gives Russalka the opportunity to chronicle as Frau Dr. Rappart her development from egocentric pietist to self-fulfillment in parenthood and marriage. However, our main interest in *Russalka* derives from its obvious link to the dramatic works. As an example of Wedekind's prose style and narrative power, it offers little else.

*Das Opferlamm* (The Scapegoat) is a bordello story. A young customer eagerly asks the prostitute with whom he is spending the evening how she came to choose her present vocation. Her story forms the main narrative line of *Das Opferlamm*, the young harlot being, in her own mind, the sacrificial lamb. As an innocent girl, she had gotten involved with a man who exploited her, driving her almost to suicide. From a feeling of disgust with herself and the entire human race, she allows herself to be sold into white slavery, in order to taste complete humiliation.

In its cynical treatment of the wretchedness of the prostitute's life, *Das Opferlamm* is the key to *Tod und Teufel*. Wedekind obviously developed the idea of a young harlot confessing her unhappiness to an interested young man first in the prose work. But there is a dimension to the young man in *Das Opferlamm* which also has significance in the development of the bizarre Mr. Tschamper from *Schloss Wetterstein*, who receives particular pleasure from watching the death agonies of others. The thoroughly depraved youth of *Das Opferlamm* has become so jaded in his association with prostitutes that he can arouse himself only if he first hears the unhappy events which led to his hostess' present debased state. But Martha, the girl of *Das Opferlamm*, has an unexpected effect on him.

Without warning, Wedekind shifts his attention to the nameless "junger Mann," as he shows the change taking place while the sad story of Martha unfolds. His cynicism turns into compassion: "He had learned to believe in innocence. He had to hate himself, whenever he thought of the young girl. Never in his life had he wanted anything good, and yet he was still not yet completely lost. He felt this. It remained with him for the rest of his life." (I, 273)

What distinguishes this otherwise trifling, and often trite, story of the good-hearted and much abused whore who saves a youth on the road to perdition is the sinister nature of Martha's urge to leap into the abyss of degeneration. Her only moments of satisfaction come when she can debase herself. There is an almost pathological desire for complete immersion in the mire of self-abuse. Martha will not go with any customer. He has to be particularly obnoxious and repulsive:

> Once a gentleman came over to me and began stroking my hair. Perhaps I would have gone with him, but he was too pleasant to me, too considerate. At the beginning Madam was not satisfied with me, because I always looked so glum. But ever since she noticed that our most disgusting customers always go with me and that I never refuse, she's been as fond of me as of Mademoiselle Palmyra. (I, 272)

This is much the same force which drives Lulu into the arms of Jack the Ripper, and which motivates Brecht's Polly Peachum in *Die Dreigroschenoper*:

> The first man who came was a man from Kent
> Who was all that a man should be.
> The second, oh, he had three schooners in the harbor
> And the third one was crazy for me.
> And as they were rich men
> And as they were nice men
> And their collars were as white as snow
> And as they knew how they should treat a real lady
> I had to say to each one: No.[2]

The dark tone hinted at in the character of Martha is more fully developed in *Der greise Freier* (The Hoary Suitor). This is a frighteningly sinister story which derives much of its power from the false start which Wedekind permits us to make. The narrative begins: "Leonie Fischer was of a fine disposition and character" and continues with a detailed description of this sensitive young Swiss girl from Lenzburg. Since childhood she has lived alone with her widowed father and sister, waiting with great patience for the right man to enter her life. She is a creature completely in control of her desires, sensitive to her own nature and responsive to the world around her. There is no problem in store for her, and when "the right man" does appear, Leonie instinctively and moderately fulfills her goals. The young people are soon engaged, then married. While on their honeymoon, as they lie in bed discussing both past and future, the young husband cannot help but comment on the seemingly total equilibrium of Leonie's nature. It is at this point that Leonie tells the story of her sister Klara, who had died not too long ago.

What follows is a startling shift of mood. The story now centers on the dark passions of Klara, a savagely formidable girl-woman whose overriding desire to marry stems from a search for tranquillity. Her passions are complicated by a morbid preoccupation with the idea that she is destined to marry an old man who could not possibly satisfy her, a thought which recurs repeatedly in Klara's dreams. Finally, she is overjoyed to find a kindred soul in Rudolph, but the lovers are thwarted from marrying one another because of Rudolph's financial situation, which dictates a long courtship.

The tension of the engagement period is overwhelming for Klara. The social restrictions of their little town demand complete propriety, and the two lovers are never left alone. The whole society seems determined to maintain the decorum of the pre-marital ritual of courtship. The hardship on Klara is too much; she has a serious heart attack. For Klara there is little hope of recovery. Her condition is grave, and to keep her alive, the doctor orders that Rudolph should not be admitted to her presence, for fear that the additional agitation might kill her. For Klara, the doctor's restriction is worse than a death sentence. Although the doctor warns her repeatedly that any physical contact with her betrothed would prove fatal, she is burning up with passion. Her dreams continue, and the nightly visitations of a blotchy-faced, wrinkled old man who comes as a suitor desiring to embrace her strengthens her resolve to disobey the physician's warning. She knows that this ancient, impotent lover is a forewarning of death; and her fate is clear in her mind. Only in Rudolph's arms can she escape. Klara begs her sister Leonie to permit Rudolph to visit her before she dies.

In Leonie's hands lies the decision whether or not to allow the two lovers to be united before death separates them. She knows what will happen if she permits them to be together. The social implications are clear; Klara would no longer be considered "ein anständiges Mädchen." Leonie is overwhelmed by the injustice she feels is being done to Klara. She cannot understand why Klara must be denied those privileges which only married women can enjoy. She agrees to arrange the meeting, and on the next morning Klara is found dead.

As the narrative returns to the honeymoon hotel room, the reader awaits the impact of this story on the young bridegroom. Wedekind for a moment suggests that there is a sense of disappointment in the controlled, dispassionate exterior of Leonie. But the young man quickly dismisses such thoughts: "He considered himself fortunate to have such a treasure of quiet contemplation, of selflessness and sacrifice, there by his side." (I, 250)

In its tone of protest against the stupidity of a repressive society, *Der greise Freier* belongs with *Frühlings Erwachen*. There is even an academic colleague of the infamous pedants of the dramatic work, a young teacher who is outraged when one of Leonie's friends appears in class wearing a skirt far too short for the delicate sensibilities of the instructor. In the midst of a lesson, the young teacher runs back to the protective sanctuary of his desk, muttering remarks about the vanity of today's youth.

Leonie herself is an unusually level-headed and realistically portrayed character. But she is still a youth really, slightly older than the teenagers of *Frühlings Erwachen*, and like them, far wiser than the world around her. She knows what society demands in the way of social restrictions; but she is not at all convinced of the justice of these demands. Her decision to leave Klara and Rudolph alone is a moral one and is intended to rebuff the social mores of her parents' generation. Yet, she herself is prepared to conform, even though she believes in the rights of others to follow a course necessary to their happiness. Leonie is perhaps Wedekind's most enlightened creature.

Throughout the entire *Fürstin Russalka* collection, Wedekind consistently demonstrates his inclination for the flashback story which frames his stories. Almost invariably, the flashback takes the form of a first-person narrative, as Wedekind instinctively moves closer to a sort of dramatic monologue in the telling of his stories, until in *Rabbi Esra* he abandons narrative exterior almost completely and creates what in effect is a play with one character. The old Rabbi addresses his son Moses, who is permitted a few words in reply; but the total effect is that of a pure monologue, with Moses no more significant than Nyukhin's off-stage wife in Chekhov's famous monologue *On the Harmfulness of Tobacco*.

In *Rabbi Esra* Wedekind has set himself a difficult task: to explore the problem of sex in the life of an elderly Jew. In spite of what seems an unlikely subject, *Rabbi Esra* is one of the most moving of Wedekind's prose pieces. The old man is upset because his son Moses wants to get engaged, yet does not even want to contemplate a marriage date. Esra insists that his son knows nothing of love; and to illustrate his own education, he tells the story of his two marriages. Like Elin in the early story *Elins Erweckung*, he had been a student of religion who was overwhelmed by feelings of sensuality. In order to curb this "gift from the devil," he deliberately selected as his bride the small and delicate Lea, in the hope of at least muting his own passions. But he was miserable with his new bride, for he felt as if he were defiling God and man alike. Yet he loved Lea dearly; and when she died two years after their marriage, he cursed God for taking her from him. Esra's reaction to what he considers an injustice from God compounded by his own guilt at not having loved Lea with total physical abandon drives him to find consolation with "die Töchter der Wüste," the local prostitutes. Like several of Wedekind's characters, he is searching for the abyss, for profound humiliation. But much to his surprise he finds no such abyss with the harlots of the town. With the total exercise of his body's powers, Esra began to bloom once again and to experience a peace of mind which he could not find with Lea in their marriage bed. His body no longer was an object of scorn, something to deprive and humble. Esra saw that his physical self had a need which had to be satisfied, and that this need was meaningful. He soon began looking for a new wife, and found an equally sensual young woman whose spiritual beauty matched her physical perfection: "Her body was the twin to my body, and her heart the brother to my heart." (I, 228) They are happily married, and Esra thanks God once again for teaching him the beauties of the senses, and that the love of God is also love of the soul's body.

The impact on Moses is difficult to determine and is left to one sentence to explain: "Moses skulked away, with his head lowered." (I, 229)

Personally Wedekind always felt that *Rabbi Esra* was one of his most satisfying works. He later dramatized it and made the little playlet a regular part of his nightclub programs. One can well see why Wedekind had this affection for a sketch of less than two thousand words. It is one of the few expressions of his belief in the union of flesh and spirit that is in no way marred by irony or skepticism. There is an honest freshness about Esra's reconciliation with himself, as well as about the apparent impact which the story has had on his son Moses.

We must not forget two very brief anecdotal tales which are expansions of passages recorded in Wedekind's diaries during his first stay in Paris. Once again, he uses his prose to test material which would later be dramatized. *Bei den Hallen* chronicles twenty-four hours in the life of the narrator, which he spends with a young Parisian girl of the streets. Most of the evening is devoted to going from bar to bar, while the girl describes several of her associates, most notably Lulu and Raimonde, a lesbian. *Ich langweile mich* (I am bored) is actually written in diary form; it consists of several entries made during a month's sojourn in Paris. The narrator, who is a writer, tells of several amorous adventures, in particular that with Wilhemine, which ends when the young lady falls madly in love with a tenor and abandons the writer. There are several autobiographical references to Wedekind's parents who are disguised as Wilhemine's parents. Her mother had spent a good deal of time in Valparaiso and San Francisco, and later lived in a mysterious castle. Having been jilted by Wilhemine, the writer falls madly in love with a young high school student named Elizabeth. In his desperation to see her, he follows the girl to school and is driven to complete distraction by her youthful beauty. By accident he picks up some of her school work and discovers, much to his dismay, that the divine creature is not particularly intelligent. Disillusioned, he retires to his apartment and contemplatively observes his cat chewing up his manuscripts.

By far the most significant of Wedekind's prose works is *Der Brand von Egliswyl* (The Fire at Egliswyl), the latest and most mature of the shorter pieces. Still another first-person story, it is clearly autobiographical, and Wedekind makes no effort to hide this fact. The narrator tells of his youth in the Canton of Aarau in Switzerland and the family mansion in the town of Lenzburg: "My father bought Schloss Lenzburg when I was eight years old." (I, 209) The town also has another significant building: the cantonal prison modeled after the newest American design! It is to this prison that the narrator takes us for the main story. In order to make repairs on the castle, his father has requested that the warden allow him to use some of the prisoners. The warden readily agrees, and the prisoners eagerly go about their work, in the meanwhile becoming quite attached to the young boy of the family, who is the narrator. Now, many years later, he is telling the story of one particular prisoner, Hans, who while walking along with him and his father, told them the story of how he came to serve a fifteen-year sentence for arson.

As in *Der greise Freier,* there is a remarkable shift in mood and temper from the outer framework story to the tale itself. Even Wedekind's prose, which is untypically realistic and discursive, and never approaches the eccentric virtuosity of much of his dramatic language, shifts in intensity. Once again the dark power of the narrative is associated with the sexual drive. The hero Hans is a male variation of the sexually starved Klara, although he apparently has found a measure of contentment denied her. He has no difficulty attracting a wealth of young girls to satisfy his needs. Like Lulu's, his origins are unknown; he does not know who his parents are. He is happily employed as a farmhand, because he understands animals and they understand him. One of his young lady friends, who takes Hans up to her room, has a vicious watchdog which, instead of attacking him, licks Hans's leg affectionately. The more amorous he becomes, the stronger the more broad-shouldered he becomes, and there seems to be no limitation to his prowess.

But Hans soon meets his match in Maria, a coquette who works in a nearby castle. She is not overwhelmed like the others and, in fact, rejects Hans's advances. He is confused, as his instincts turn to infatuation. He becomes a moon-sick lover, begging Maria for a sign of love. He is humiliated and, like Moritz Stiefel, even contemplates a flight to America. Hans is unable to eat, work, or sleep; but at the very moment when his grief is greatest, Maria relents and allows him to come to her room. Here he experiences the final, degrading humiliation, for the efforts to win Maria have taken a tremendous toll: he has become impotent. Maria contemptuously drives him out of her room. Only after he has been left alone with his terrible humiliation does his passion return to him. In a rage of boundless fury, Hans finds only one way to prove his masculinity to Maria, and he sets fire to the entire village.[3] When he returns to tell Maria of his triumph, she ignominiously turns him in to the authorities.

Wedekind's stories have a strong impact on the person who happens to be the listener. In *Der greise Freier, Rabbi Esra,* and

*Das Opferlamm,* the final tension results from the change in the attitudes of the listener which the story has brought about. In *Der Brand von Egliswyl,* there is a peculiarly subdued reaction, which is softened also by the time elapsing between the actual telling of the story by the prisoner and the narrator's decision to tell it to us: "Actually I didn't really understand what the significance was until many, many years later. By now the prisoner must be already a free man." (I, 219)

In this story, Wedekind comes closest to paralleling Strindberg's particular attitude toward the female. In general, it would be safe to state that whereas Strindberg was a confirmed denigrator, Wedekind was just as firm an admirer of women. But in this single narrative Wedekind demonstrates a Strindbergian misogyny. Maria systematically attempts psychologically to emasculate the otherwise uncomplicated and contented young farm lad. She is diabolical, and the contest is unequal from the start. Wedekind's conception of her is that of a representative of society's unhealthy repressions, since she controls and contains Hans's instincts until he is driven wild. But in spite of this suggested bias, Wedekind is careful enough not to allow it to intrude too overtly into the telling of the story. He allows Hans's naïvete and Maria's destructive teasing to speak for themselves; and in a coolly ironical manner, aided by the framework, the author remains detached from the action. The arsonist tells his story in his own words; and Hans's simple language, like that of Büchner's *Wozzeck,* mirrors his true nature, while the language of the frame is much more elevated and stylized. The total effect is, as Victor Lange suggests, reminiscent of the classic Kleistian novella, "no less powerful and no less frightening."[4]

Wedekind's remaining shorter prose works merit at least brief mention. *Die Liebe auf den ersten Blick* (Love At The First Glance) appeared in *Die Fürstin Russalka;* and while artistically of no great consequence, it is another expression of Wedekind's esthetic of motion. At a social gathering a man has a brief encounter with an attractive young lady and astonishes her by making a proposal of marriage. He contends that he knows all there is to know about her, because he has seen her walk. The rhythm and smoothness of her movement reveals the perfection of her soul. The girl is soon convinced and accepts the proposal. Wedekind's preoccupation with bodily movement stems from his early interest in the circus; and the particular act of walking formed always a main part of his doctrine. In *Der Liebestrank* it dominates the entire play, and in

*Die Büchse der Pandora*—besides the obvious significance of Lulu's career as a ballerina—there is the fact that Jack the Ripper spots Lulu on the streets of London when he notes the uniqueness of her walk.

Both *Flirt* and *Die Schutzimpfung* (The Vaccination), neither of which appeared in the first collection, are trivial and erotic little episodes. *Bella, eine Hundegeschichte,* is an often witty tale of the love of two little dogs. *Der Verführer* (The Seducer), which was published only after Wedekind's death, is the most interesting of the "Nachlass" prose, the material found posthumously in Wedekind's notebooks. The narrator, a pedantic young scholar of the classics, describes his successful quest for the affection of a young lady who was actually willing to be conquered. She first teases him, then draws him on, hoping that he will take the hint that she is ready to submit. But our academician is too preoccupied with his studies to notice the obvious suggestions which the girl is making. She drags him out into the garden of her home, pulls him down on a secluded bench, leans over, and while stroking his hair, asks him what is is thinking about. "I'm thinking about the Greek inscriptions on the monuments in western Asia Minor," he replies. They finally manage to get their signals straight, and eventually marry.

Wedekind's only novel remained a fragment, although it appeared in print as early as 1901. *Mine-Haha* is a novel of education, Wedekind's personal statement of how to bring up young women. It is a Utopian, purely theoretical novel, and Wedekind admitted that he considered it "a daydream, not concerned with the question of feasibility." The framework is unique. An elderly woman has committed suicide and has instructed her legal adviser to hand over the manuscript to the author of *Frühlings Erwachen.* Wedekind then proceeds to read this account.

The central figure is the old woman, Hidalla, who recounts her memories of an extraordinary childhood education. She is capable of recalling events as early as her second year of life. Until the age of seven, she spent her days in delightful play with her six friends in a lovely house surrounded by beautiful woods and flowers. Their mentor was a girl named Gertrude, who instructed them in running, walking, swimming, and various other kinds of physical activity. They were hardly ever clothed and did not receive shoes until the age of four. At seven the girls were separated. Hidalla was placed with still another group of girls in a large brick house, one of thirty buildings set in a magnificent park. All the girls wore flimsy white dresses and received more advanced training in physical education, augmented now by instruction in dance and music.

Hidalla develops an infatuation for her instructress, the beautiful Simba, who represents for the young girl physical perfection itself. Instruction is always under the direction of the oldest girl in the house, and the adult world is completely shut out. The girls' only formal education is in the principles of beauty. Hidalla has her first contact with the outside world when she performs in the school's theater, before an audience of outsiders. The children perform Wedekind's *Der Mückenprinz,* and Hidalla discovers that through such performances the school maintains itself. As the audience leaves by the exit door in the rear of the auditorium, Hidalla's curiosity about this strange, unknown world is awakened for the first time.

At the age of fourteen, Hidalla is given the responsibility of educating a group of younger children. Finally, with her own education completed, she is led outside through the theater and, together with twenty-five other girls, is taken to the railroad station. There they meet the same number of young men, and hand in hand they march through the town accompanied by the universal applause and jubilation of the citizenry.

For all of its apparent idiosyncrasies, this strange paean to physical fitness is one of Wedekind's most sincere statements. His own commitment to bodily perfection was no less sincere. According to Kutscher Wedekind himself was a practicing nudist, weightlifter, and gymnast. He actually became a sort of symbol to the great number of physical-fitness societies which were springing up all over Europe, and especially in Germany. Kutscher tells us of an invitation extended by the Hellerau School in Switzerland to see some of his ideas put into practice.[5] This was deadly serious business for Wedekind, because he conceived of *Mine-Haha* as the most reasoned argument against the charges of obscenity which were still being leveled against him. His children's world is, for the most part, wholesome, if one will forgive the erotic ballet, which is, after all, meant for the jaded and genuinely obscene outside world. Wedekind tried to show innocence in its most delightful form and felt pride in bodily beauty. If this was eroticism, concluded Wedekind, it was not bad, for it was not obscene. In Wedekind's mind, there existed a clear demarcation between these two concepts. In the essay "Über Erotik," which serves as an admirable introduction to *Mine-Haha,* he outlines his thoughts on this matter: "It is an insane crime systematically to educate the youth of our nation with stupidity and ignorance in respect to matters of sex, and systematically to lead them to a dead end." (I, 200) Society does this, he continues, by calling whatever has to do with the body obscene. "Obscenity is a mockery, a denigration, an insult to sexuality." (I, 205) In *Mine-Haha*, Wedekind attempts to demonstrate the innocence of bodily pleasure and sexuality, which is naturally implied as the group of young people walks through the town displaying the perfection of their physical existence. He reminds his audience of an old saying by suggesting that it might apply to it: filth is in the mind of the beholder. For Wedekind, as far as his novel is concerned, the utopian world of the children is blissfully wholesome.

## CHAPTER 10

# *The Place of Frank Wedekind*

WEDEKIND wrote much that can be called mediocre; but in a half-dozen plays created during one decade of his life, he anticipated many techniques to be found today in the modern theater of revolt, a concept of drama which Robert Brustein says, "rides in on the dark fury of Nietzsche, with his radical demands for a total transformation of man's spiritual life."[1] Inspired by a passionate hate for the tepid sociology of the Naturalists, Wedekind almost single-handledly initiated an onslaught against every vested interest of middle-class existence. He destroyed the ordered world which the everyday citizen could recognize and replaced it with one that was fiercely distorted, without order or authority, and thoroughly devoted to the advocacy of a new civilization.

During this brief span, Wedekind made war on everything connected with tradition, both in society and in the theater. As Artaud expressed it almost fifty years after Wedekind, what was missing from civilization was meaningful myth; not the tired Christian or Greco-Roman myths, but a pre-logical, primitive, self-gratifying force. In Lulu, Wedekind had thought that he had created a force which conceivably could alter the development of civilization. In Genet, Ionesco, and Cocteau, mythic material has become the very foundation of their art, and once again it is "the dark sexual freedom" which Wedekind explored in his Lulu plays.

At the roots of Wedekind's revolt was his hostility toward the conventional civilization which he found all around him. His passionate discontent determined the focus and scope of the revolution he would attempt in the theater.

He loved to portray mankind in a state of mental aberration, brutally obsessed with a violent desire to destroy everything that was natural and beautiful. Wedekind assaulted society at its most sensitive points—marriage, family, sexual morality—and then perpetrated the final insult. He forced these respectable citizens to mingle on stage with a bizarre collection of knaves, prostitutes, and sundry raffish types who were far outside the boundaries of "nice" society. Not only that, but Wedekind did not give his characters a chance to speak for themselves. In concentrating on what Camus calls "the divorce between man and his life which constitutes the feeling of Absurdity,"[2] he had to create a new style for the stage, a form which in its technique, language, and effect has been known in Germany as "Der Wedekind-Stil," and which has been the fore-runner of much that is of consequence in the German theater today.

From the outset, the central controlling force of Wedekind's plays was Wedekind himself. The author was placed squarely in control of characters and action, without even the slightest genuflection to the ability of the characters to act for themselves. Their psychological state of mind was a matter of complete indifference to Wedekind; they were puppets, created to do the bidding of the puppeteer. Their personalities have little or no basis in reality; they act out of no normal motivation, and their distortions are not the product of inner psychological tensions, but impositions stuck on by Wede-kind's ubiquitous hand.

Obviously, Wedekind saw the need for a new means of communi-cation—or non-communication—between these one-dimensional creatures. The result was a new linguistic phenomenon, a language that exists nowhere else except in the mouths of Wedekind's charac-ters, an often ferociously aggressive lyricism fused with the awkward banalities of the most trivial everyday speech. Wedekind's characters rarely use language for the purpose it was intended, i.e., communi-cation. They address themselves, speaking for personal consumption in an utterly non-discursive, often surrealistic fashion.

On top of this, Wedekind placed his marionettes in grotesque situations which could underline his view of society. He channeled his ideas in a fashion to produce an image of society staggering stupidly to its own destruction. For this the traditional vision of tragedy was insufficient and not in keeping with the author's scorn. What was needed was a new sense of mockery, indeed, of humor. Wedekind's characters literally clown on the road to perdition; or, if they are permitted for a moment to take themselves seriously, he will see to it that the rug is pulled from underneath them.

For this dehumanized civilization Wedekind wanted a dehuman-ized, a non-traditional theater. He preferred the atmosphere of the circus with its animals and transformed the staid Victorian parlor into a training ring, a microcosm of man in his bestial state. He opened the theater to song, pantomime, and the dance in an effort to free society from its inhibitions and to force it to recognize its primitive origins.

Above all stood Frank Wedekind, like Genet, searching for martyrdom, belonging and not belonging, disconnected from a society which he detested; but which he desperately wanted to help, "Der Niggerjud," as he called himself, the most isolated of possible men.[3] Like Dietrich Christian Grabbe before him, he had prepared himself for the role of the rebellious, alienated artist whose tragedy was that he was in advance of his time.

## I  *Influence*

On February 2, 1916, the Cabaret Voltaire opened in Zurich, and the Dada movement was born. The first program included a reading of Alfred Jarry's *Ubu Roi*, written in 1897, a savagely hilarious attack on middle-class man, which has become a classic of the literature of revolt. On the same program appeared songs by Frank Wedekind. The Dadaists were among the first to embrace Wedekind. No less than he, they were dedicated to the overthrow of Western values and created their own brand of literary anarchy. They destroyed the accepted limitations of the theater and substituted pure, undiluted imagination. Out of everything offensive to the everyday world they amalgamated an outrageous theory of insult. The first concrete absorption of Wedekind's ideas can be seen from the play which is recognized as the prototype of Dadaist drama, Oskar Kokoschka's *Sphinx und Strohmann*, written in 1917 and revised in 1919 as *Job*. At the heart of Kokoschka's apocalyptic play is the conflict between man and woman, very much in the Wedekindian manner. Job, the simple-minded man, is incapable of dealing with the female force represented by Anima, Kokoschka's version of Lulu, who boldly deceives her husband at every turn. Throughout the plays of the Dada period, numerous "Lulus" emerge, each one imbued with a positive charge which destroys the uncomprehending male.[4]

For the writers who are bunched together under the heading of the German Expressionists, Wedekind's influence was perhaps even more direct. Acknowledged inheritors of the unique Wedekind prose style were Carl Sternheim and Georg Kaiser, whose messianic, often hysterical language is a logical outgrowth from Wedekind's dialogue. For the German Expressionists, the man Wedekind was as important as his art. They viewed him as the persecuted prophet, a tragic victim of society's refusal to accept the truthfulness of the creative vision. The cult of Wedekind began in the early 1920s and lasted through the hectic days of the Weimar Republic.

For the National Socialists, Wedekind was, of course, the epitome of decadence and artistic sickness. The fundamental Puritanism of the Nazi mentality reacted as violently as had the rigid formalism under the Kaiser. His plays were removed from the stage, his works not republished. An entire generation grew up ignorant of Wedekind; but when after almost twenty years of sterility the German intellectuals began searching for a mentality which had battled those forces which led to National Socialism, they found in Wedekind's grotesquely black humorous vision of mankind the most accurate image. In Friedrich Dürrenmatt's cynical satires the Wedekind influence is unmistakable. The bizarre menagerie of *Der Besuch der alten Dame* (*The Visit*) and its sordid distortion of values could have come from several of Wedekind's plays. In Max Frisch—like Dürrenmatt, a Swiss—is found the same sense of caricature and farce which is the mark of Wedekind's tragic slapstick. Again, the presence of Wedekind himself had a particular impact on these two writers. Both had gotten their earliest training in the Zurich cabarets like the Cafe Voltaire. It was in such places where Wedekind was given some of his greatest hearings, especially since Zurich was for him an adopted city. His own activities as a nightclub entertainer made him all the more attractive to the habitués of these clubs, and Frisch and Dürrenmatt are two of the most illustrious graduates of this school of entertainment which Wedekind, more than any other literary figure, made respectable.

## II *Wedekind and Brecht*

Upon no other writer has Wedekind left such an indelible mark as on Bertolt Brecht. Even the most cursory examination of their lives, theories, and techniques demonstrates to what considerable extent Brecht accepted Wedekind both as his personal and ideological mentor. This was no academic literary influence comparing two writers who lived thousands of miles apart, and in different ages, such as Ibsen and Arthur Miller or Strindberg and Eugene O'Neill. In the case of Wedekind and Brecht, there was a very tangible, personal, and physical impact which bordered on hero worship on the part of the young Brecht during his student days in Munich in 1918. At that time Wedekind had already gained the stature of a great and venerated man, certainly as far as the political and artistic avant-garde were concerned. The sudden swing to patriotism had been shrugged off by many of his followers as a brilliant ploy to deceive the censor. He was still the pariah of properly civilized people, and as such still the elder statesman of the Bohemians. Wedekind, on his part, did not separate himself from his followers, in spite of the respectability and stability which his marriage and children brought him. He continued to sing in the literary cabarets of Munich which were frequented by the young writers and artists of the city, one of whom was Bert Brecht. Brecht himself gives an account of the physical impact Wedekind made on him:

He had only to enter a lecture-room with hundreds of noisy students, or a room, or a stage, with his special walk, his sharp-cut bronze skull slightly tilted and thrust forward, and there was silence. He filled every corner with his personality. There he stood, ugly, brutal, dangerous, with close-cropped red hair, his hands in this trouser pockets, and one felt that the devil himself couldn't shift him.[5]

The impact which this aging actor and writer had on a young student-writer named Bert Brecht lasted during the latter's entire life. The director Kurt Hirschfeld, a friend and professional associate of Brecht's, wrote in 1962 to Günter Seehaus:

Brecht was a great admirer of Wedekind's, and above all of his manner of acting. You are quite right in suggesting that he took much from Wedekind. One of his favorite subjects of conversation was Wedekind, and whenever he talked about him, he would try to imitate how Wedekind had played the role of Dr. Schön.[6]

Wherever the youthful Brecht went in Munich, he encountered Wedekind. In the nightclubs, the lecture halls of the university, and the professional stage, Wedekind's presence was considerable, and Brecht seemed to search him out. He attended Kutscher's theater history classes, in the hope of hearing one of Wedekind's frequent readings there.

Even the superficial and most likely coincidental similarities between the lives of the two men strikes one as startling. Like Wedekind, Brecht began his association with the Bohemian fringe early in life. Also, he had a childlike fascination for the circus, and even paralleled the Wedekind-Rudinoff relationship by his association with the great Munich clown and impersonator Karl Valentin. Like Wedekind, Brecht was an outspoken pacifist, who was not above compromising his ideals in the best tradition of self-preservation. Finally—and one is tempted to think here of a conscious imitation—Brecht gained a reputation as a singer of songs as well as a guitarist and lutenist, talents which were, like Wedekind's, self-taught.

From the outset, Brecht was a literary disciple. His earliest verse was distinctly derivative of Wedekind's own poetry, which unfortunately, because of limitations of space, cannot be considered in this study. The brutally cold, grotesque objectivity, the almost clinical eroticism which are found in Wedekind's *Schauerballaden,* murder songs, and street-singer poetry are echoed in Brecht's early lyrics. Brecht's first play, *Baal,* written in the year of Wedekind's death, is a reworking of Wedekind's Lulu plays.[7]

Like Wedekind, Brecht abandoned traditional subject matter for a non-Christian myth. Baal is a Phoenician fertility god, a symbol of primitive, erotic force and a male counterpart of Lulu; he is a representation of primal innocence and moral irresponsibility, beyond guilt or judgment, and the instinctive enemy of social morality. Their sexual instincts reflect their universality, for both Lulu and Baal are bisexual, attractive to both sexes. Baal, like Lulu, is consciously stripped of what one would call normal psychological character. He feels no remorse for his victims, nor does he triumph.

In the end, Baal is also destroyed, the victim of a similar social order which, out of necessity for survival, must exterminate this force. The similarity in allegorical treatment is carried over into language as well. Brecht's "symbolism of decomposition" is the natural extension of Wedekind's animal imagery.[8] In both cases the universe reacts to the energy which Lulu and Baal generate, and man is reduced to the animal state: the hunter animal, the predator, chases his victim, until he catches him and destroys him. Baal, as Walter Weideli has stated, is, along with Lulu, an animal in heat, and must be satisfied.[9]

It was only natural that Brecht would outgrow the ideology of Eros that is reflected in *Baal;* for his creative powers were not nearly as limited as Wedekind's. As his Marxism more and more intruded into his dialectic, he gradually shifted his central point of interest. Yet in *Lux in Tenebris* (1919) the clear presence of the Wedekind morality is still very much in evidence, reflecting much of the same irony as is found in *Tod und Teufel.* It is also a "bordello-play."[10] A law-abiding gentleman named Paduk sets up an exhibition opposite a brothel aimed at demonstrating the dangers of venereal disease. The madame, after listening to Paduk's passionate attack on universal vice, soon succeeds in convincing Paduk that his genuine interests would be better served in partnership with her. Paduk forgets his morality in a hurry and goes into business with the quick-witted Madame Hogge. The brutal cynicism is vintage Wedekind, as is the tone, image, and language.

By the time Brecht wrote *Die Dreigroschenoper* (1928), his Marxist commitment was fairly well established, so that his main concern was to place Macheath properly in the economic structure of London's underworld. Nevertheless, the "hero" is still a gay variant of Wedekind's Jack the Ripper, transformed by Brecht into a happy-go-lucky lust murderer.

One particular treatment of a theme by Wedekind remained a constant part of Brecht's frame of reference, and that was the image of America. Unlike Wedekind, Brecht eventually did get the opportunity to observe the New World at first hand. But in the years before his travels took him to America he had already developed a vision of the United States which apparently could have come from no other source but Wedekind; for it was Wedekind who first distorted that image. As we have said, at times Wedekind had shown some admiration for America as a land of social freedom and opportunity, and there is sufficient evidence to indicate that he genuinely wanted to return to the country which his parents had adopted. At times, Brecht also was capable of showing considerable regard for things American. In the poem "Verschollener Ruhm der Riesenstadt New York" ("Forgotten Glories of the Giant City of New York"), Martin Esslin detects an undertone of awe and nostalgia.[11] In *Der Flug des Lindberghs* (1928) the flight of the American aviator is looked upon as a triumph of intelligence and Yankee ingenuity.

But it is the "American Dream" of the capitalist which would naturally dominate Brecht's attitude, and he found in Wedekind's grotesque Americans a ready-made source of inspiration. Pierpont Mauler of *Die Heilige Johanna der Schlachthöfe* (*Saint Joan of the Stockyards*, 1929), is an offprint of Wedekind's villainous businessmen, except that Mauler spouts Americanisms because he is indeed an American—with a peculiarly American-German name. For both Wedekind and Brecht, Chicago represented American depravity at its worst. In *Im Dickicht der Städte* (*In the Jungle of the Cities*, 1921), a play which, like Wedekind's *Bethel*, depicts a fantastically exotic dream-America, *Happy End* (1929), and *Der aufhaltsame Aufstieg des Arturo Ui* (*The Resistable Rise of Arturo Ui,* 1941) Brecht shows no inclination toward a merely realistic and less grotesque interpretation, although one of these plays was written during Brecht's stay in America. As in Wedekind, there is always a feeling of remoteness, even naïvete in Brecht's grimly sordid view of America's midwest.

Numerous critics have hinted that Brecht's "Epic Theatre" is not really as revolutionary as had been thought originally, and it is often startling to see the extent to which Brecht's development of theatrical theory is based on Wedekind's ideas. Wedekind was the first modern German dramatist to reject Aristotelianism in the theater, and his specific attacks on the Stanislavskian style of acting, as exemplified in his own peculiar style, became, as has been noted, the model for Brecht. Every one of Wedekind's staging devices was meant to detach the audience from the reality of the situation, to alienate his spectators. He created roles which puzzled the traditional actors of his generation, and he wrote specifically for the purpose of creating a new style of performance.[12] The vehicle itself, the play, was for Wedekind a means of educating by demonstrating in a highly personal way the stupidity of life, by showing the audience what stupidity was like. Wedekind reduced everything to the ridiculous, constantly reminding his viewers that this was not life as it is, but as it should not be. His plays are distinctly *Denkspiele,* much as Brecht called his own plays *Lehrstücke.* It was in Wedekind that Brecht found his purpose in the theater, and the mode in which to express this purpose.

In his obituary of Frank Wedekind, which has already been quoted, Brecht described him as one of the great educators of modern Europe. This is a point well worth noting, when we consider his increasing claim for attention as an innovator in a nation which, during his lifetime, was singularly non-iconoclastic. He disturbed, shocked, and irritated a society which wanted no part of him and his imaginative extravagance. Ultimately, he lost his magic. But during the few years of significance for him and for the modern theater, he served as the bridge between the forgotten revelation of Büchner and Grabbe and almost single-handedly saw to it that experimentation and irreverence remained a part of German drama. Now, fifty years after his death, the modern theater once again finds Wedekind's disjointed world in tune with its own.

# Notes and References

## Chapter One

1. Herbert Marcuse, *Eros and Civilization: A Philosophical Inquiry into Freud* (New York: Random House, 1955), p. 3. The most relevant books by Freud in their consideration of man and the civilization which he has constructed are: *A General Introduction to Psychoanalysis* (New York: Garden City Publishing Co., 1938), *Beyond the Pleasure Principle* (New York: Liveright Publishing Co., 1950), and *Civilization and Its Discontents* (London: Hogarth Press, 1949).

2. Frank Wedekind, *Gesammelte Werke in neun Bänden* (Munich: Georg Müller Verlag), IX, 149. Because of inconsistencies in the use of acts and scenes, reference to the *Gesammelte Werke* will be by volume and page.

3. For an excellent discussion of the over-all development of Wedekind's perspective, see Walter H. Sokel, "The Changing Role of Eros in Wedekind's Drama," *German Quarterly*, XXXIX (1966), 201–7.

4. Marcuse, p. 85.

## Chapter Two

1. Ernst Hoferichter, "Sonderlinge und Originale," in *Denk ich an München*, ed. Hermann Proebst and Karl Ude (Munich: Gräfe und Unzer Verlag, 1966), p. 107.

2. "Frank Wedekind," in *Brecht on Theatre*, edited and translated by John Willett (New York: Hill and Wang, 1964), p. 3.

3. Quoted from Artur Kutscher, *Frank Wedekind. Sein Leben und seine Werke*, I (Munich: Georg Müller Verlag, 1922), 19.

4. For a more complete discussion of Wedekind's parents, see Oskar Seidlin, "Frank Wedekind's German-American Parents," *American-German Review*, XII (1946), 24–26.

5. Frank Wedekind, *Gesammelte Briefe in zwei Bänden*, ed. Fritz Strich, I (Munich: Georg Müller Verlag, 1924), 316.

6. Because of the nature of the material, all the poetry will be left in the original.

7. I, 144.

8. *Briefe*, I, 179.

9. *Ibid.*, p. 176.

10. See Frederick Heuser, "Gerhart Hauptmann and Frank Wedekind," *Germanic Review*, XX (1945), 54–68.

11. Quoted from Klaus Völker, *Wedekind* (Velber bei Hannover: Friedrich Verlag, 1965), pp. 16–17.

12. Kutscher, II, 13.

13. As a political thinker and personality, Wedekind was one of the most outspoken literary figures of his generation. Essays advocating abolition of the death penalty, reform of the penal code, and intelligent dissent by the press, clearly placed him in the camp of the civil libertarians. His pacifism was an accepted fact known to everyone. Helene Stöcker, writing in *Die neue Generation*, noted: "As a pacifist Wedekind was openly outspoken before 1900. Indeed, he anticipated the most significant attitudes of our time." XIV (1918), 97.

14. Quoted from Kutscher, II, 119.

15. See Günter Seehaus' exhaustive

study of the critical reception in *Frank Wedekind und das Theater* (Munich: Laokoon Verlag, 1964), pp. 28 ff.

16. *Ibid.*

17. In the Seehaus compilation there are listings of every production of Wedekind's plays through 1964.

18. See Pamela Wedekind, "Mein Vater Frank Wedekind," *Der Kammersänger* (Stuttgart: Reclam, 1959), 59–66.

19. Wedekind considered his essay "Über Erotik" his personal vindication of the charge of obscenity which was constantly hurled at him.

20. The very same journal carried several articles protesting the honor suggested for Wedekind. In the first two August issues Ernst Greiner strongly opposed any such award: "His ideal is a condensation of all the decadence of our age, his works a mirror of debasement."

21. XII, 636ff.

22. Theodor Seidenfaden, *Der Gral,* XIII (1918), 59ff.

23. These essays are printed as one in *Gesammelte Werke,* IX, 417.

24. *Denk ich an München,* p. 109.

25. "Eine Szene von Wedekind," *Frank Wedekind: Prosa, Dramen, Verse in zwei Bänden,* I (Munich: Georg Müller-Albert Langen Verlag, 1960), 16.

## Chapter Three

1. Many critics have taken note of the Büchner-Wedekind kinship, but perhaps the most graphic illustration of it is found in Alban Berg, the genius of atonality who died in 1935, and whose two major works were the operas *Wozzeck,* based on Büchner's play, and *Lulu,* the libretto for which Berg synthesized from Wedekind's *Erdgeist* and *Die Büchse der Pandora.* More than any literary figure, Berg saw the relationship between the two writers. See H. F. Redlich, *Alban Berg, The Man and His Music* (New York: Abelard-

Schuman, 1957), pp. 74–111, 163–202.

2. A very useful study of Büchner, which gives special attention to his influence on Wedekind, is Herbert Lindenberger, *Georg Büchner* (Carbondale: Southern Illinois University Press, 1964).

3. For a consideration of the Freudian implications of the money-making instinct and its relationship to eroticism, see Norman O. Brown, *Life Against Death* (New York: Alfred Knopf, n.d.), pp. 234–304.

4. Kutscher, I, 170.

5. Count Schneinitz' entire character and function were taken without any alteration from one of Wedekind's favorite plays, Christian Dietrich Grabbe's *Scherz, Satire, Ironie und tiefere Bedeutung* (1822), in which one Baron von Mordax appears as a delightfully lecherous nobleman.

6. *Frank Wedekind, der Mensch und das Werk* (Jena: Erich Lichtenstein, 1920), p. 28.

7. Quoted from Völker, p. 16. In a later edition of the play, Wedekind omitted these lines, which do not appear in subsequent editions.

## Chapter Four

1. Wedekind was not the only dramatist to deal with this theme. Both Max Halbe's *Jugend* and Gerhart Hauptmann's *Hanneles Himmelfahrt* treated the problems of youth sympathetically before the turn of the century.

2. *Wedekind,* 27.

3. The translations of these names are taken from *Spring's Awakening,* translated by Eric Bentley, in *The Modern Theatre,* vol. 6 (New York: Doubleday Anchor Books, 1960), p. 6.

4. *The Grotesque in Art and Literature,* tr. Ulrich Weisstein (New York: McGraw-Hill, 1966), p. 131.

5. *Ibid.,* p. 133.

6. *The Playwright as Thinker* (New York: Reynal & Hitchcock, 1946), p. 64.

7. *The Changing World in Plays and Theatre* (Boston: Little, Brown, 1939), p. 42.

8. I, 249.

9. Concerning the similarity between Büchner and Wedekind, Kayser notes: "This aspect of Wedekind's play actually strikes us as being familiar, for the teachers who hold a conference in *Frühlings Erwachen* strongly remind us of the captain and the physician in Büchner *Woyzeck*," *op. cit.*, p. 131.

### Chapter Five

1. "Was ich mir dabei dachte," *Gesammelte Werke*, IX, 426.

2. Since 1945 *Der Liebestrank* has become one of the most popular works in the German repertory and has enjoyed some of the most imaginative productions found on the stage. Elaborate musical scores for circus orchestra or jazz ensemble have been written, and sets constructed which place the audience inside a circus tent! See Seehaus, pp. 254–60.

3. Nietzsche's name appears in a startling number of instances throughout Wedekind's works, and in *Die Büchse der Pandora* he is referred to as "the most divine genius of the dance that the world has ever seen."

4. *Gesammelte Werke*, VI, 315–33.

5. The only place in the complete edition where this work is found is in the novel *Mine-Haha*, I, 317–81.

6. *Gesammelte Werke*, VI, 337–75.

7. Freudian critics would no doubt be interested in Wedekind's treatment of the medical profession in his works in light of his father's vocation. In every instance, the characterization is of a thoroughly inept, utterly bumbling stereotype.

8. *Gesammelte Werke*, IX, 67–132.

9. A more considerable treatment of Wedekind's impact on twentieth-century writers will be given in a subsequent chapter.

10. *Frank Wedekind: Ausgewählte Werke*, Ed. Fritz Strich (Munich: Georg Müller, 1924), I, XXXVIII.

11. Wedekind continued to use "no-talk" characters even in his dramatic works, as did Kafka in "In der Strafkolonie" (In the Penal Colony), a short story which makes considerable use of pantomime. Wedekind's ballets are also strikingly reminiscent of a new form of entertainment which was just beginning to establish itself: the silent movie.

12. *The Theatre of the Absurd* (New York: Doubleday Anchor Books, 1961), 278.

13. Translated from the French by Mary Caroline Richards (New York: Grove Press, 1958), p. 110.

### Chapter Six

1. See Seehaus, pp. 337–434.

2. All quotations from *Erdgeist* and *Die Büchse der Pandora* are from *Five Tragedies of Sex*, translated by Frances Fawcett and Stephen Spender, introduction by Lion Feuchtwanger (New York: Theatre Arts Books, n.d.), pp. 97–302.

3. Fechter, p. 45.

4. *The Playwright as Thinker*, p. 64.

5. *The Writer in Extremis* (Stanford, California: Stanford University Press, 1959), p. 63.

6. See Marcuse, p. 12.

7. See Freud's *A General Introduction to Psychoanalysis*, p. 273.

8. Otto Rank, *The Trauma of Birth* (New York: Harcourt, Brace, 1929), p. 93.

9. See Sokel's "The Changing Role of Eros in Wedekind's Drama," *loc. cit.*, p. 205.

10. Wedekind made this point in defending himself from the charge of obscenity which the government lodged against him. In the prologue to a post-trial edition of *Pandora* he wrote: "The tragic central character of this play is not Lulu, as was mistakenly assumed by the judges, but

the countess Geschwitz," *Gesammelte Werke*, III, 102.

11. Within the span of a few years, Wedekind's view of the prostitute changed radically, from the idealization of *Das Sonnenspektrum* to the frightening realism of *Pandora* and the subsequent *Tod und Teufel*.

12. Marcuse writes: "The function of sadism is not the same in a free libidinal relation and in the activities of SS troops. The inhuman, compulsive, coercive, and destructive forms of these perversions seems to be linked with the general perversion of the human existence in a repressive culture. . . . ," *Eros and Civilization*, p. 185.

13. Artaud, p. 31.

14. *The Theatre of Revolt* (Boston: Little, Brown, 1964), p. 367.

15. See Siegfried Kracauer, *From Caligari to Hitler* (New York: Noonday Press), pp. 48–50, 153–80.

16. *Ibid.*, pp. 160–61.

17. Of all the literary figures who associated with Wedekind, Heinrich Mann was perhaps the most intensely loyal. His most graphic tribute to Wedekind appeared in a volume of memoirs published in 1929, *Sieben Jahre*.

*Chapter Seven*

1. *The Writer in Extremis*, pp. 55–82.

2. A term used to describe the tormented state of mind of the Expressionist writers by Jakob Wassermann, "Offener Brief," *Die Neue Rundschau*, XXI (1910), 999.

3. Several of Wedekind's closest friends, as well as his daughters Pamela and Kadidja, have commented that Wedekind was at his happiest when living the life of the solid burgher. After his marriage and the arrival of his children, he established a fairly rigid discipline in the family, and in general acted the role of a devoted husband and father. See Pamela Wede-

kind, "Mein Vater Frank Wedekind" in the Reclam Edition of *Der Kammersänger*.

4. "Eine Szene von Wedekind," *loc. cit.*, pp. 10–16.

5. Obviously the publishers saw the connection between the aphoristic style of Nietzsche and Wedekind. The title of the collection was *Also sprach der Marquis von Keith*. It was published in 1902 by the journal *Die Jugend*.

6. Critics have also noted the similarity of style between Wedekind at his most epigrammatic and the great English epigrammatist Oscar Wilde. A 1967 production of Alban Berg's *Lulu* in Düsseldorf emerged as *The Picture of Lulu*, as if it had been conceived by Wilde rather than Wedekind. See *Opera News*, April 1, 1967, p. 32.

7. See "Der Wedekind-Stil der Bühne" in Seehaus, pp. 701–9.

8. Sokel, *The Writer in Extremis*, pp. 55ff.

9. For a consideration of Wedekind in the tradition of the "lonely poet" in German literature, see Kasimir Edschmid. *Über den Expressionismus in der Literatur und die neue Dichtung* (Berlin: E. Reiss, 1919), pp. 19ff.

10. Wedekind appears to have been the first German writer to make the insane asylum a major motif in his work. The theme is central to modern writers such as Günter Grass (*The Tin Drum*), Erich Maria Remarque (*The Black Obelisk*), Peter Weiss (*Marat/Sade*), and Friedrich Dürrenmatt (*The Physicists*), to mention just a few.

11. See *Briefe*, I, 217 and "Anmerkungen," p. 352.

12. Quoted from *Deutsches Theater des Expressionismus*, Ed. Joachim Schondorff (Munich: Georg Müller-Albert Langen Verlag, n.d.), p. 13.

*Chapter Eight*

1. Quoted from Seehaus, footnote, p. 30.

2. *Frank Wedekind, der Mensch und sein Werk*, p. 111.

3. See Adolf Rudolf Vieth, "Die Stellung der Frau in den Werken von Frank Wedekind," unpublished dissertation, Vienna, 1939.

4. Sokel, "The Changing Role of Eros in Wedekind's Drama," *loc. cit.*, p. 204.

5. "Was ich mir dabei dachte," *Gesammelte Werke*, IX, 434.

6. Wedekind in a letter to Alfred Kerr, Berlin, 1908, in *Briefe*, II, 212.

7. Voelker, p. 56.

8. *Ibid.*

9. *Frank Wedekind und das Theater*, p. 179.

10. The edition published by Bruno Cassirer, for example, contained almost fifty pages of text taken from the court minutes.

11. See L. R. Shaw, "Bekenntnis und Erkenntnis in Wedekinds *Die Zensur*," *Frank Wedekind zum 100. Geburtstag*, herausgegeben von der Stadtbibliothek München (1964), pp. 20–35.

12. "Was ich mir dabei dachte," pp. 434ff.

13. See "Frank Wedekind" in Ludwig Thoma, *Gesammelte Werke*, neue erweiterte Ausgabe in acht Bänden, I (Munich: Piper Verlag, 1956), 260–63.

14. See Seehaus, pp. 357ff.

15. See Sokel, *The Writer in Extremis*, p. 60.

16. This and the following translations from *Schloss Wetterstein* are taken from Fawcett and Spender, *Five Tragedies of Sex*.

17. Kutscher, III, 112.

18. Fechter, p. 124.

19. See Seehaus, pp. 683–93.

20. Joachim Friedenthal's defense of Wedekind's position comes in the "Nachwort," "The contradictions . . . are not such to those who knew him. They stem . . . from his great pleasure . . . at tricking the censor," *Gesammelte Werke*, IX, 467ff.

## Chapter Nine

1. With one notable exception. Wedekind's *Der Brand von Egliswyl* appears in *Great German Short Novels and Stories*, edited, with an introduction by Victor Lange, Modern Library Edition (New York: Random House, 1952), pp. 387–95.

2. Translated by Guy Stern, for Columbia Records Release of *Die Dreigroschenoper*, 1958.

3. Freud draws several interesting parallels between pent-up sexual frustration and the urge to commit arson. See *Psychopathology of Everyday Life* (New York: New American Library, 1951).

4. *Great German Short Novels and Stories*, xix.

5. Kutscher, II, 131.

## Chapter Ten

1. *The Theatre of Revolt*, p. 8.

2. *Le Mythe de Sisyphe* (Paris: Gallimard, 1942), p. 18.

3. In several of his uncompleted works, Wedekind deals with the character of "Der Niggerjud," an idea which occupied his mind from 1896 to his death. In a sense, he is the composite of all of Wedekind's facets, the blending of the Hauptmann-Wedekind dichotomy, "the werewolf," as Wedekind also described him. See *Entwurf zu einem Drama mit dem geplanten Titel Taugenichts* and *Der Werwolf*, *Gesammelte Werke*, IX, 245–89.

4. See Martin Esslin, *The Theatre of the Absurd* (New York: Doubleday Anchor Books), pp. 229–89.

5. *Brecht on Theatre*, trans. John Willett, p. 3.

6. Seehaus, p. 707.

7. Universally it has been accepted that Brecht's main idea in writing *Baal* was to parody Hanns Johst's Expressionistic play *Der Einsame*, aiming to ridicule the image of the poet as seer.

8. See Herbert Lüthy, "Of Poor Bert Brecht," *Encounter*, XXXIV (1956), 33–53.

9. *The Art of Bertolt Brecht,* trans. Daniel Russell (New York: New York University Press, 1963), p. 6.

10. The theme of the "world as a brothel" is given its most contemporary expression in Genet's *The Balcony.*

11. "Brecht's Language and Its Sources," in *Brecht,* ed. Peter Demetz (Englewood Cliffs, New Jersey: Prentice-Hall, 1962), p. 177.

12. Wedekind's most important essays on the art of acting and theory of drama are: "Schriftstellar Ibsen und *Baumeister Solness,*" "Begegnung mit Josef Kainz," "Schauspieler," "Was ich mir dabei dachte," and "Vorrede zu *Oaha,*" *Gesammelte Werke,* IX, 291ff.

# Selected Bibliography

PRIMARY SOURCES

*Gesammelte Werke in neun Bänden,* ed. Arthur Kutscher and Joachim Friedenthal. Munich: Georg Müller, 1919–24.

*Ausgewählte Werke in fünf Bänden,* ed. Fritz Strich. Munich: George Müller, 1924.

*Prosa, Dramen, Verse.* Two vols. Munich: Georg Müller-Albert Langen, 1960–64.

*Ich habe meine Tante geschlachtet, Lautenlieder und Simplizissimus—Gedichte.* Munich: Georg Müller-Albert Langen, 1967.

*Gesammelte Briefe.* Two vols. Ed. Fritz Strich. Munich: Georg Müller, 1924.

*Der vermummte Herr: Briefe Frank Wedekinds aus den Jahren 1881–1917.* Ed. Wolfdietrich Rasch. Munich: Deutscher Taschenbuch Verlag, 1967.

SECONDARY SOURCES: SELECTIVE

Bentley, Eric. *The Playwright as Thinker.* New York: Reynal & Hitchcock, 1946.

————. "Bertolt Brecht's First Play," *Kenyon Review.* XXVI (1964), pp. 83–92.

Blei, Franz. *Über Wedekind, Sternheim und das Theater.* Leipzig: Kurt Wolff, 1915.

Block, Anita. *The Changing World in Plays and Theatre.* Boston: Little, Brown, 1939.

Block, Haskell and Robert Shedd. *Masters of Modern Drama.* New York: Random House, 1962.

Brustein, Robert. *The Theatre of Revolt.* Boston: Little, Brown, 1962.

Esslin, Martin. *The Theatre of the Absurd.* New York: Doubleday & Company, 1961.

Fawcett, Frances, and Stephen Spender, trans. *Five Tragedies of Sex,* intr. Lion Feuchtwanger. New York: Theatre Arts Books, n.d.

Fechter, Paul. *Frank Wedekind, der Mensch und das Werk.* Jena: Erich Lichtenstein, 1920.

Garten, Hugh. *Modern German Drama.* New York: Grove Press, 1962.

Gundolf, Friedrich. *Frank Wedekind.* Munich: Georg Müller-Albert Langen, 1948.

Guthke, Karl S. *Geschichte und Poetik der deutschen Tragi-komödie.* Göttingen: Vandenhoeck & Ruprecht, 1961.

Hill, Claude. "Wedekind in Retrospect," *Modern Drama,* III (1960).

Kayser, Wolfgang. *The Grotesque in Art and Literature,* tr. Ulrich Weisstein. Indiana University Press, 1963.

Kutscher, Artur. *Frank Wedekind: Sein Leben und seine Werke.* Three vols. Munich: Georg Müller, 1922–31.

————. *Wedekind, Leben und Werk,* adapted and edited by Karl Ude. Munich: List, 1964.

Seehaus, Günter. *Wedekind und das Theater.* Munich: Laokoon Verlag, 1964.

Sokel, Walter. *The Writer in Extremis.* Stanford University Press, 1959.

————. "The Changing Role of Eros in Wedekind's Drama," *German Quarterly.* XXXIX (1966).

Spalter, Max. *Brecht's Tradition.* Baltimore, Maryland: The Johns Hopkins Press, 1967.

Völker, Klaus. *Wedekind.* Velber bei Hannover: Friedrich-Verlag, 1965.

*Wedekindbuch, das.* Munich: Georg Müller, 1914.

*Wedekind, Frank: Zum 100. Geburtstag.* Ed. Stadtbibliothek Munich, 1964.

# Index

## Index